60 Million Illegal Aliens in America!!!

A simple, America-first solution.

Donald Trump's signature issue from the announcement of his presidential candidacy has been immigration reform because he loves America and Americans. As difficult as it is for good, hard-working Americans to believe, our government has been working to keep us poor. Former President Obama's de-facto amnesties and a do-nothing Congress made it tough for Americans to find work while competing against foreign interlopers.

Congress has been lying and yet their efforts have produced a terrible truth—Americans have been left behind and nobody cares. Meanwhile, uninvited guests, working for peanuts, have reduced wages and taken the few jobs that exist today. After they get here, these poor souls languish in misery and a lifetime of poverty as even what they take from our welfare system is hardly enough, Reviewers of this plan will be able to see that the Resident Visa Plan will help Americans first and that it is also designed to help illegal foreign nationals in have a better life also. They will no longer be chained to greedy businesses looking for slave-labor wages.

The Resident Visa Plan takes interlopers out of the shadows and gives them opportunity. If well-behaved, they gain the right to stay and work in America for a lifetime, one year at a time. They will be out of the shadows with no amnesty, no citizenship, no freebies, no line jumping; and no jobs before Americans.

These goals are satisfied in the Resident Visa Plan and for those who would rather a jump start back in their home country, The Stipend Return plan puts money in their pockets as soon as they arrive in their home country. These two plans are destined to save America a half-Trillion dollars each year.

Those who sign up for the program must be vetted every year and must pay a fee each year or be deported. There's lots more! You're going to like this America-first plan built by an American for Americans. Any questions?

BY

Brian W. Kelly

LETS GO PUBLISH

AF797650

Title: 60 Million Aliens in America Is a Big Problem
Copyright © 2017 Brian W. Kelly
Publisher: Brian P. Kelly
Author Brian W. Kelly

Published by: LETS GO PUBLISH!
Editor Brian P. Kelly
Email: info@letsgopublish.com
Web site www.letsgopublish.com

Library of Congress Copyright Information Pending

Book Cover Design Brian W. Kelly
Publisher Brian P. Kelly

ISBN Information: The International Standard Book Number (ISBN) is a unique machine-readable identification number, which marks any book unmistakably. The ISBN is the clear standard in the book industry. 159 countries and territories are officially ISBN members. The Official ISBN For this book **978-1-947402-13-3**

The price for this work is: **$12.95**
USD

10 9 8 7 6 5 4 3 2 1

Release Date: October 2017

LETS GO PUBLISH!

Dedication

Each & Every day when I would go to work in the front office, and sometimes even before I would arrive, my two co-workers on every other book project were there to greet me and work with me all day—other than for extremely necessary bio-breaks for all parties.

This book is dedicated to these two fine individuals Benny, the first little man, passed away on Thanksgiving last year after a fine stuffest but his spirit continues with me. Buddy does his best to make up for Ben's absence.

Ben *& Dad*

Buddy*, Ben & Mom*

Acknowledgments:

I appreciate all the help that I have received in putting this book together as well as all the other 128 books from the past.

My acknowledgments were so large at one time that readers complained that they had to go through too many pages to get to page one.

And, so I put my acknowledgment list online, and it continues to grow. Believe it or not, it costs about a dollar less to print my books today than then. No kidding!

Thank you, my dear friends and supporters of many years. May God bless you all for your help.

You may check out www.letsgopublish.com to read the latest version of my heartfelt acknowledgments updated for this book.

A new lover of literature, Wily Ky Eyely continues her supportive efforts.

Thank you all very much!

Brian

Preface:

What would you call a plan that solved a problem for America that most of the Congress seems to have no interest in solving? I have called it many things while perfecting this book, but now let me settle with what I would like to call ***The Stipend Return / Resident Visa Plan***.

I had called the plan many things but never hit the nail on the head. This is my vision for a secret sauce solution to fix the problem of 60 million interlopers waking up in America every day. Yes—build the wall, please! But simultaneously solve the residence problem of so many people who do not belong here. Do we really need up to 60 million interlopers in residence? I do not think so. Hey, John McCain thinks there are over 128 million interlopers in residence. What now?

There are many problems with illegal immigration today. For the United States, the biggest problem is the fact that the cost of welfare, cash payments, and medical assistance is bankrupting the country. We cannot afford the huge cost that illegal interlopers place on our system when most of them collect some form of welfare.

Every resident feels about a $1500 burden from the generous plans that help illegal residents survive in America's shadows. Additionally, wages for Americans are always going down while expenses are going up. The new Stipend Return / Resident Visa program solves both of these problems at the same time.

I am happy that you are reading this book and I hope many others find it and convince the Administration and the Congress and the President that it is their turn to learn about The Resident Visa Plan.

This book is the result of over ten years of work from way back when I wrote my first patriotic book in 2006 titled Taxation without Representation. Version three of this book is now current. The Resident Visa Plan was formalized in 2013 under a different title.

At the time that this work evolved to its current shape, I had examined everything out there especially the Gang of Eight Plan (GO8), existing law, and other notions about how anybody might possibly solve the nation's concerns about 60 million illegal residents.

At first look, I found no real solutions other than either amnesty or follow the law: deportation. The Resident Visa solution is unique and everything needed to implement it is already in place.

The Resident Visa solution directly addresses the issues that having 60 million illegal foreign nationals in residence have brought upon America. One other approach rewards illegal activity and makes everybody OK and is a bad example, and another approach gives most people a bad, sinking feeling in their gut. That's why nobody has come forward to suggest that 100% deportations are really a good idea for the country at this point.

Deportation is fair of course as these folks have broken our laws. But, our politicians are culpable as they made it too easy for foreigners to break our laws. Amnesty is not a solution as Americans have already paid a big price for the largesse of politicians wanting low wages and those wanting the future votes of today's interlopers.

Ideally, the solution would be to go poof, and every foreign interloper would be taken back to where and when they crossed the border years and years ago. Where is a used Star-Trek Transporter when we need one? This time, however, they would not be re-admitted if they tried to cross. The fact is that the problem never should have reached the level of severity that it is today. Nobody can perform miracles and tricorders are not invented yet so when we have the closest ingenious thought to a miracle as a solution, we should examine it and embrace it.

After defining the problem in my early books, I developed a methodology that would make Americans pleased and would remove all interlopers from the shadows—and into the light of the American day or back home with some cash in their pockets if they choose.

Americans in this system would have priority and for their right to participate, interlopers would agree to pay their own way while in our country. Such a plan ought to work. Only the bad guys would be deported.

When I carefully read the Gang of Eight "comprehensive" plan in 2013, I noticed that it smelled a lot like it was purposely designed to kill America. No jobs would be left for Americans. Newly unemployed Americans would have to pay for newly minted citizens getting a lifetime of freebies. We would see them voting in national elections; and watch their numbers grow until there were 33 million more foreign nationals looking for jobs by plan—jobs that Americans cannot even find.

Per Heritage.org, the cost for the 33 million that were intended to be brought in by reunification provisions of the Gang of 8 Bill, was estimated at well over $6 Trillion. Even Donald Trump does not have that much money. I think. The bottom line is that this was a terrible deal for the country.

I was hunting for a real immigration fix that pleased Americans. Marco Rubio, Chuck Schumer and the rest of the Gang of Eight were looking for scalps to prove to Democrats that they had the progressive agenda in the forefront. Let me tell you now folks. I do not. Like they did in the 1920's, progressives are again trying to undermine America.

I looked at all the things that Americans want in a real plan—things they liked and things they do not like. I wanted interlopers to embrace the plan so they could get out of the shadows without hurting Americans. So, among other things, I examined what interlopers liked about living in America.

In my first cut at solving the problem in 2013, I figured out a way to permit well-behaved interlopers to stay in America one year at a time with a realistic annual renewal fee, while giving Americans priority in all ways. It was a good plan but not as perfect as I had hoped. The biggest problem with the plan was that it was difficult to explain in clear concise terms.

I was convinced that the plan actually would work and that it would solve the problem for the long haul and take a huge financial burden off the backs of Americans. And, so, I kept at it, continually improving it until it was perfected.

Every plan requires fine tuning and we would expect this to continue to be the case with the Resident Visa Plan. By implementing the current iteration of the plan, the long-sought solution to the result of illegal immigration is around the corner.

To see what US officials on the pro-American side of the issue would think about such a plan for America, I contacted Pennsylvania Congressman, Lou Barletta. Many know Lou Barletta as a tireless advocate for fighting illegal immigration and amnesty. He is running for the Senate against a very poor legislator, Bob Casey, Jr., in my state of Pennsylvania. I presented a detailed PowerPoint of my ideas in late January 2015 to the Congressman and his chief aid at the time, Joseph Gerdes. After perfecting the plan even more, I reached out again and presented in 2016 to the Congressman.

The Congressman was most pleased with my presentation and the detail that backed up each and every point of the presentation. The Congressman and I continued to engage in a lengthy dialogue on these issues. We spoke about the difficulties in getting immigration legislation for Americans through the House and the Senate, and he updated me as to where the Congress was with some new initiatives in securing the border.

During this interchange, the Congressman helped me understand what was really happening in Washington. For my part, I helped the Congressman to fully understand the benefits of this immigration fix for as many as 60 million foreign nationals residing illegally in America.

Both Congressman Barletta and President Trump have made the wall and border security their # 1 priorities. This plan addresses those who are here now. I am sure we could do both at the same time.

My strong recommendation to Congressman Barletta and President Trump is that we add this immigration fix, which I call “The Resident Visa Plan,” to the "Beautiful Wall" and the Bills and the Amendments on Border Security. This would be the best anybody could do to solve the problem of resident interlopers in America once and for all.

This would be the first comprehensive and comprehensible immigration plan ever put forward that favored America and Americans over foreign nationals. It is America-First.

I sent the Congressman a text version of the presentation with its new logical flow so that he could take it, read it, and share it without having to figure out the hidden messages within the bullets of a PowerPoint. This new update will be in Senator Barletta's hands before it is on the street for sale.

As I examined the document that I produced, I realized that it was much more complete than the original Kelly Plan. Its sequencing was much better; and the additions from the Barletta presentation / interview added a lot of missing pieces to the package. And, so, I decided to re-work the text document to make it even better.

In 2013, Americans rejected the Gang of Eight Amnesty Bill. So, here I am again, in my 129th book writing again about the problem of 60 million interlopers making it tough for Americans. This time, however, it is far more simplified and easier to implement.

A key element of this plan is that each year the clock resets on foreign nationals who are permitted here under the Resident Visa Plan. This book, thus focuses on interlopers signing up to become Resident Visa Holders with appropriate renewal assurances for good behavior.

This is ***the*** tool to accomplish the goal of an America and American-First solution to 60 million interlopers. There are a lot of other adjunct notions besides the Resident Visa Plan such as a solution for visa over stayers, green card holders, as well as a unique solution for current birthright citizens.

The solution for the illegal interloper issue is large enough to warrant its own book. President Trump already has a team of people working on other solutions in the immigration umbrella such as border security and the wall, visa overstays, sanctuary cities and other issues not directly related to the 60 million interlopers taking from Americans every day.

You won't believe how easy the problem of 60 million interlopers is to solve if we can get our legislators to take action or President Trump finds he can take Executive Action.

In summary, this book presents the Resident Visa Plan as the fix and the Stipend Return Plan as a backup fix. Then it offers many other points on why this is the one and only fix to create an America without shadows that favors Americans 100%. There is so much good left over that good-willed interlopers have a lot to gain simply by signing up.

I wrote this book to help Americans know what our President and Congress can do to force our government to regain control of our borders, ensure our national security, keep our culture, enforce our laws, protect American jobs, make our language the language of the nation, and keep all Americans from being overwhelmed by illegal foreign nationals who offer few benefits and no allegiance to America.

In addition to showing why amnesty is not the right medicine, I take the time to explain in detail the best plan for America to again become a sovereign state with America-loving Americans in charge.

You are going to love this book as well as the plan itself. All interlopers immediately are to be registered and accountable. You will see that The Resident Visa Plan (SR/RV) is designed by an American for Americans.

Additionally, illegal foreign nationals will be very pleased because the plan uses deportation as a very last resort and it immediately gets illegal foreign nationals out of the shadows. Few books are a must-read but *60 Million Illegal Aliens in America Is a Big Problem* will quickly appear at the top of America's most read list. It also has a catchy subtitle:

This is a simple, America-first solution if Congress and the President have the guts! It solves the problem!

Table of Contents

About the Author

Brian W. Kelly retired as an Assistant Professor in the Business Information Technology (BIT) program at Marywood University, where he also served as the IBM i and midrange systems technical advisor to the IT Faculty. Kelly has designed, developed, and taught many college and professional courses. He is also a contributing technical editor to a number of IT industry magazines, including "The Four Hundred" and "Four Hundred Guru" published by IT Jungle.

Kelly is a former IBM Senior Systems Engineer and he was a candidate for US Congress from Pennsylvania. He has an active information technology consultancy. He is the author of 128 other books, in many topical areas, as well as hundreds of articles. Kelly has been a frequent speaker at many US conferences. Invite him to your next conference on immigration solutions.

When Kelly ran for Congress as a Democrat against a 13-term Democrat in 2010, he took no campaign contributions, spent just enough to buy signs and T-shirts, and as a virtual unknown, he captured 17% of the vote. Kelly says: "Writing books is lots easier than running for public office!"

Chapter 1 The CliffsNotes Version

60 million interlopers in 60 seconds

I do not have to go far out on a limb to suggest that if we knew how to immediately stop the drain on our government treasuries with one bold and very fair move, our representatives would be forced to adopt the measures necessary to achieve the gains. In this case, it would be to stop the major treasury drain that occurs each and every day to support a population segment of illegal interlopers. The term interloper, whether legal or illegal means *uninvited guest*.

Based on what it costs to support illegal foreign nationals. we can certainly afford to deport millions of people. However, there are many good reasons why we should not deport anybody other than criminals. Most of the 60 million illegal residents are hardworking and living quiet, orderly lives. We also cannot allow them, as a result of their illegal entry, to become citizens. This would violate the basic premise of following the rule of law that is a key standard of citizenship. This book offers two great solutions to solve this bog problem.

By the way, in this abbreviated "CliffsNotes" chapter, Cliff had nothing to do with the notes. However, *CliffsNotes* is easily recognized for being what they are. Everybody seems to know they are a series of student study guides available primarily in the United States. The guides present and explain literary and other works in pamphlet form or online. Of course, if Cliff wants to produce a CliffsNotes version of this chapter or the entire book, he is more than welcome to do it and if he would like, we will create a new Chapter 1 for his new work.

I predict that the biggest obstacle in solving the problem of 60 million illegal interlopers in America will be both chambers of the US Congress. I am not naïve enough to suggest that the current Congress' predilection for more voters and lower wages for all

Americans could be overcome by the fact that this plan to deal with resident interlopers is the best yet conceived. So, we may be forced to replace them all in order to do the right thing for America.

We cannot let our corrupt Congress get in the way of our solving our problem with the 60 million. I admit that this would probably be more difficult than stopping the treasury loss but at least we would all know what we must do, and seeing Congress packing would be a pleasure to the senses.

John McCain is known for his estimate of a clip of about 4 million per year. Illegal aliens (interlopers) have chosen to cross the southern border or they have chosen to simply overstay their visas in order to gain residence in the US. Amnesty advocate John McCain, who is a recognized authority on the subject of illegal immigration, in a letter dated February 2004, wrote that apprehension figures demonstrated that "almost four million people crossed the US border illegally in 2002."

McCain estimates over 10,000 cross every day. Adding it up, that comes to 128 million by the end of 2017. If we cut that in half and round it down, we're looking at my estimate of 60 million interlopers in residence today. I know that nobody can prove me wrong.

The name of the plan to solve the problem of 60 million interlopers makes sense when you think about it. It is the *Stipend Return / Resident Visa Plan*. The little slash means *or* in this case. The program immediately takes 60 million illegal foreign nationals out of the shadows and saves the US treasury a minimum of a half-Trillion dollars each year after year 1. Should Congress and /or the President pursue this plan? Of course!

What problem does the program fix? It is a pro-America and pro-American citizen solution. It is an America-First solution to the major problem of 60 million illegal residents sponging off the taxpayers in the United States. Once in the continental US, the interlopers either wholly or partially depend on US taxpayer dollars for their daily sustenance. Is your wallet looking a little thinner these days? The problem we plan to solve in this book, *the real problem,* is that 60 million illegal foreign nationals cost Americans money every day. They just don't pay their way and live here. They take from US.

Should any plan include sending 60 million illegal aliens back home?

Maybe!!!

Maybe we should send them back if that is what they want. It is my contention that we lured them into America by giving them the idea that the streets were paved with gold and when they took their share of that gold, the streets would grow more gold. They are culpable for sure but our politicians deceived them by not building a wall and by not enforcing our border protections.

Because of the role of corrupt American politicians in their coming here, there was an implicit promise that illegal interlopers could stay and we Americans would make sure they were OK. Because of America's role in bringing them here, I would say that we owe them at least a free trip home with a little pocket money. But, we can afford a lot more and it would serve us well if we paid it.

Yes, you heard me right. We need to pay for their return 100% and give them some pocket money. A full-boat fake-id welfare recipient can actually cost taxpayers in 2017 about $30,000 per year so giving interlopers a large sum to go home is very business-prudent.

The Stipend Return program is built for those interlopers who want to leave the US with a few bucks ($20,000) in their pockets. We can afford to package a nice stipend of at least $20,000 per person willing to return home. In other countries, this type of stipend is called pay to go and is becoming very popular especially for refugees in Europe who are being paid to go.

Under the US Stipend Return program, the former interloper receives the ½ the sum from a bank in their home country when they get back home and the other half one year later. Of course, all of this is if that is what they want. They cannot return to the US.

If they want to stay in America, that too is OK but the terms will be American terms to which they must agree.

The US savings on the Stipend Return is easy to calculate. A $150,000 cost over five years is very substantial if the interloper decided to stay in America. A $20,000 stipend would be substantially less than the five-year cost and we would have to pay it just once.

So, it makes sense to pay for the costs of departure and to give those illegal foreign nationals who choose to leave on their own accord not only a free ride home but a wad of cash too. The$20,000 stipend in my humble opinion is key to make the offer fair and proper and cost-effective.

It will help the former interloper to reestablish themselves in their home country with a nice nest-egg. This can be their starting point for prosperity in their country of origin. It is win-win. If they do not wish to leave, so it stands.

Americans win and illegal residents also win when they decide to go back home to live. In the event that officials determine that $20,000 is not enough for an attractive incentive, we can up the amount to what is necessary, knowing that if an interloper on a free lunch program stays twenty-years, the cost for Americans may be as high as $600,000.00 There is a lot of stipend room between $20,000 and $600,000. We're looking at US payments of $1.8 million per person for a 60-year lifetime resident.

What if interlopers do not want to go home

If a resident illegal foreign national really does not want to go home regardless of the incentive, then there is another option that actually costs taxpayers nothing and permits the interloper to stay in America indefinitely in a legal state as long as they "behave." The program provides for granting interlopers in good standing what we are about to call a Resident Visa. This is a new visa type that, unlike other visa types can be renewed each and every year with conditions.

With this, former foreign nationals would be legal under the protection of the Resident Visa and could remain in America as long as they behave in a lawful manner according to the exact terms of their visa.

There are many differences between illegally gaining benefits in the United States and becoming legal by gaining a Resident Visa. Those choosing to employ the Resident Visa to stay in America, are welcome to do so; but the terms of the relationship with US officials will not be the same as when they were illegal.

For example, there are no more cash incentives. The former interloper will be temporarily legalized after applying for a special US passport and then a Resident Visa and after being approved for both. The visa will be special in that it will be renewable with a fee of $100 required annually after a renewal application, a record update (demographics, etc.), and a re-vetting of the applicant, and a special oath of allegiance.

There are major benefits to the former foreign national for going through this process. The Resident Visa holder will receive an official photo ID at their application source so they do not have to carry a passport or an accompanying visa.

For those familiar with the notion of American visas, this unique visa permits those approved, to live in America as long as they want, and as long as they renew their Resident Visa each and every year. In essence, this process provides a Resident Visa, an official US visa. Like all other visas, this provides all of the benefits of a US non-immigrant category visa and more.

The liberal progressive ideology has a habit of taking words and making their usage appear to be, for want of a better word, bad. There is nothing intrinsically wrong with the word illegal, and there is nothing intrinsically wrong with the word, alien. Moreover, when the term illegal alien, as used in US immigration law, is used in everyday speech, there is nothing implied that makes the term disrespectful to the person who fits the description. It is merely a statement of fact that permits an individual to be identified and described with accuracy without caring about their name.

What types of US Visas are there?

The type of visa that a visitor or traveler must obtain is defined by U.S. immigration law, and relates to the purpose of the travel. There is one new category of visa proposed for current illegal alien US residents in addition to the two main categories in existing U.S. law:

1. **Nonimmigrant visas**– For travel to the USA on a temporary basis.
2. **Immigrant visas**–For travel to live permanently in the United States.
3. **Resident visas**–New--For current resident aliens to live temporarily in the US on an annually renewable basis.

Visitor Visa

Generally, a citizen of a foreign country who wishes to enter the United States must first obtain a visa, either a nonimmigrant visa for temporary stay, or an immigrant visa for permanent residence. A prerequisite for a visa just about everywhere in the world is a passport.

Visitor visas as they are called is a type of nonimmigrant visa for persons who want to enter the United States temporarily for business (visa category B-1), tourism, pleasure or visiting (visa category B-2), or a combination of both purposes (B-1/B-2).

The Resident Visa would be similar to the Visitor Visa but it is intended for those who have become residents illegally and the US wishes to make the situation right.

Description of the new visa category

Under the new Resident Visa Program, a third type of visa will be authorized by US officials. It is called a *Resident Visa*. Current law says all visa holders must first have passports containing information such as their home country and other pertinent information. The new visa category will also require a passport.

The new visa category is intended for those residents formerly in an illegal status, who register for and are granted a Resident Visa. Unlike other visas, the Resident Visa may be renewed annually as long as the holder does not violate the terms of the visa.

Like all visa requests, the individual must first possess a passport and then apply for the Resident Visa. The costs for the resident passport and the Resident Visa would be the same as under current law. An additional charge may be added to the visa fee for an ID card so the Resident Visa holder does not have to keep the passport and visa on their person at all times. The visa is renewable annually for a $100 fee to reflect changes such as address or marital status etc. The ID card and picture must be refreshed every five years.

Since the new program in its entirety, would provide for the voluntary egress of illegal aliens as well as providing Resident Visas for those who choose to stay, this is a combination plan. An interloper would get to execute just one of these options. If the program were fully adopted by US officials as law or as an Executive Order, a proper name would be: Stipend-Return / Resident Visa Program.

For discussion purposes, this can be referred to as the SR/RV Program. However, the part that most Americans will want to learn to assure that they are getting a fair shake from the government is the Resident Visa Program. The Stipend Assisted Return Plan is fairly self-explanatory. My opinion is that it will remain the quiet part of this revolutionary program. Despite its serendipitous presence, it is such a great deal for both parties that it will save the US the most treasury tax dollars.

Years ago, a friend of mine told me about an experience he had with an IBM Executive that proved to him that business deals were like a marriage. Both parties must bring something desirable to the table. The Stipend Return / Resident Visa Program does exactly that.

At the end of the day, the United States will have no more resident aliens. Instead, the former illegal interlopers will either have gained a Resident Visa and be legalized and be under the terms of the visa or they will be in their home countries cashing their massive stipend check while preparing to knock them dead as a newly funded entrepreneur in their home country.

Pro-American Comprehensive Immigration Program

We have already described this as *the Stipend Return / Resident Visa Program*.

Will this be enough to prompt Congress and the President to finally create a comprehensive immigration plan that is pro-American? It depends on what's in it for Americans and what is in it for Foreign National Interlopers? Let's examine the benefits for interlopers first as those reading this book may not see those many advantages first.

If the illegal alien population does not like this plan, it will die on the vine as leftists create a narrative that helps push a thought that it is demeaning for illegal residents to accept a Resident Visa when the illegal resident can simply push harder and perhaps get citizenship by decree from weak politicians.

Of course, there will be a fight, but if a majority of legislators can say to Americans that this plan is fair. It does not upset the delicate voter balance in this country and it does not place illegal foreign national workers, once legalized, in front of Americans, I think our best legislators on both sides can get this passed.

In the next area of this chapter, I outline the major benefits for today's shadow-living illegal foreign nationals who do not want to live in the shadows for their entire natural lives. Following this, since there are so many benefits for the currently illegal community, I outline the most salient reasons why Americans should be "all-yes" for the Stipend Return / Resident Visa Program. There are lots of benefits for all Americans. Let's start this monologue below:

There are many benefits for those living in the shadows, who want a sense of belonging and an opportunity to succeed in America.

Think about why an illegal alien residing in America in the shadows should like the Stipend Return / Resident Visa Program? While you are thinking, consider the fourteen points below.

Why should an illegal alien residing in America in the shadows find either of these two different plans acceptable?

- ✓ **Stipend-Assisted Return Program**
- ✓ **Resident Visa Program**

1. No more living in the shadows of America.
2. Opportunity to go home travel-free if desired with a big stipend paid by Americans.
3. US will budget $15 Billion for safe cities in home countries for returning immigrants
4. US will develop 15 safe settlements / cities with 10 in Mexico
5. Can get in line (back of line) in home country for citizenship without leaving US.
6. With renewals, the opportunity to live in America a lifetime.
7. Can obtain a driver's license, insurance, etc.
8. Can keep any job that is already held.
9. Can apply for any job available in America.
10. Can live wherever they want in America.
11. Can get same paid by patient medical insurance as Americans.
12. Can get installment loans from US Government on an exception basis to help with medical and educational expenses. Must be paid back.
13. After five years but no more, living with a Resident Visa, can still opt for stipend to go home.
14. Anchor family stipends to go home are huge ($50,000 per birthright citizen) and cumulative with a no-return promise.

I would suspect that list above provides a lot more advantages for interlopers than most would ever believe from how the corrupt US press will preview this program. Yet, this is just one of two major options that under the Stipend Return / Resident Visa Program, from which illegal residents may choose.

Many of the advantages for current interlopers are listed in the fourteen points above. The first plan provides a pay-to-go option that is more generous than any other country in the world. The second plan is the Resident Visa Program since getting a Resident Visa is all that is needed to win the illegal alien game. If you want to win and stay in America, this is the plan for you.

Winning the illegal alien game thankfully does not mean that Americans are shut out. Any illegal foreign national who opts for the stipend deal and departs for home under the Stipend-Assisted Return Program should have no regrets as all expenses are paid and the stipend is nice, and it includes $20,000 for each alien dependent who are also in the program. A three-child family can provide a $100,000 stipend for the family in the home country and the US can more than afford to pay it.

Knowing this is so beneficial to interlopers, why should Joe America want this program? In a nutshell, it is because Joe America is smart and knows this will save a ton of dollars for him and all Americans.

Many Americans do not trust the government, period. So, why would Americans think this is a good deal if the illegal foreign national does not choose to exit America with a stipend? Then what?

If an illegal foreign national chooses not to accept this US government act of kindness, and does not go home, and does not sign up for The Resident Visa Program—the only two options in the Stipend Return / Resident Visa Program, there is only one course of action left for the government. The interloper will be asked to leave the country at their own expense. They will be deported otherwise.

By the enactment of this new visa and this new "return home" plan, the idea of residing in America in an illegal alien status is being eliminated, period. The lack of a decision by an illegal interloper to choose one or the other will unfortunately provoke immigration authorities to deport them.

Why should an American citizen like these two plans?

1. The days of the free lunch are over.
2. Fee based passport & Resident Visa is designed to be cost free to Americans
3. Return Home stipends pay for themselves in one year
4. Illegal aliens must agree to terms of Resident Visa-- all benefits eliminated after 1st year.
5. Once an illegal alien returns home, cannot come back; no cost is accrued after year 1

6. No birthright citizenship for illegals, permanent residents, and Resident Visa Holders
7. No cash, medical services, education, welfare, or other benefits permitted for those with a Resident Visa.
8. No citizen-only privileges permitted
9. Resident Visa Holders have no right to vote in any election
10. New jobs must go to American citizens first—all things being equal.
11. Fees, fines on employers will help pay for Resident Visa program kickoff. Will generate approximately $400 Billion.
12. When program in high gear, US will save more than $500 Billion per year on interloper expenses.
13. Resident Visa holder must be employed (1 yr. to get a job)
14. Resident Visa holder must have self-paid or employer-paid healthcare
15. Resident Visa holder must pass English test in two years
16. Resident Visa holder must take oath of allegiance to be approved for 1st renewal
17. No more green cards for family reunification-instead use Resident Visa.
18. All green card permanent residence visas are eliminated when expired. No new green cards. Use Resident Visa.
19. Next 10-yr green card renewal becomes a Resident Visa
20. No path to citizenship without going home to get in line (begin a process like all others from that country)
21. Citizenship line -- jumping the line is not permitted.
22. Major cost savings for America

The end of Sanctuary Cities

Victor David Hanson writes: "Sanctuary cities protect illegal aliens from federal immigration agencies in a way that is not true of American citizens who arrive at airports and must go through customs, with no exemption from federal agents examining their passports and personal histories. If crimes or infractions are found, there is no safe space at an airport exempt from federal enforcement."

The SR/RV program either pays illegal interlopers to go or it provides a Resident Visa that offers many benefits to both interlopers and American citizens. For example, it saves about $500,000,000,000 per year after year one of its implementation. With no more illegal aliens in the country, a major advantage is that the divisive notion of Sanctuary Cities and the term Sanctuary Cities can be removed from the US vocabulary. There will be no need for them with residents all being legal.

Anchor babies qualify

The Stipend Return program is also available to those who became citizens through the anchor baby loophole of the 14th amendment. When an Anchor child with parent chooses to join the Stipend Return program, each anchor citizen child will receive a $50,000 stipend and each of his or her interloper parents will receive their own $20,000 for a total of $70,000 for a two-person family and $90,000 for a three-person family with one child. A family of four children with a mom or dad would receive $240,000. With mom and dad, the sum would be $240,000. This is very affordable for US citizens considering the lifetime cost of one anchor baby can be as much as $2 million or more.

DACA "children" also qualify

The SRRV program solves the problem for DACA children also. DACA children qualify for the full $20,000 stipend in the Stipend Return Program. Those in the DACA program also qualify for the Resident Visa Program if they want to stay in the US. As an additional DACA concession for the "Children" who opt for the Resident Visa, there will be no charge for the visa for the first five renewal years. DACA "children" will be vetted when they apply for a resident passport. Gang members, of course, will be deported without benefits.

The evidence is on the table.

Nobody in their right mind wants life to continue with a shadow population who in many ways have been victimized similar to how slaves were victimized many years ago. The Stipend Return and the Resident Visa are programs that provide a way out of the mess for both interlopers and regular Americans.

Greedy fat cat business persons and politicians at the highest levels created this mess for both factions. Consequently, the plan includes substantial fees and fines for those businesses who hired illegal interlopers instead of Americans. Being greedy will cost the fat cats over $400 Billion and perhaps more. They made a ton of money of the backs of Americans with lower wages while poor interlopers were living in squalor with sub-minimum wages. American industry as represented by the Chamber of Commerce should show some remorse and voluntarily chip in to help solve this problem and back the Stipend Return / Residence Visa Plan as it is a winner for all decent Americans and the long-suffering communities whose only solace is the shadows of America.

Quick Comparison with the Gang of Eight

In 2013, eight US Senators known as the Gang of Eight got a bill passed in the Senate that sold Americans down the river and would have given a ton of benefits to illegal aliens at taxpayer cost. The Stipend Return / Resident Visa Program is pro-American and saves taxpayers substantial dollars. It is nothing like the John McCain / Marco Rubio Gof8 sellout. It is explained in detail later in the book. For now, the following quick comparison chart is shown to help us better understand the new combined program by comparing it in the chart below with the Gang of Eight Program

2013 Gang of Eight v Resident Visa

	G of 8	SR/RV
Border secure	No	More technology
Jobs	Favors Interlopers	Favors Americans
Amnesty	Yes	No
Path to citizenship	Yes	No (almost same as today)
Permanent residents	Yes	Never, renewable visa
Voting	Yes	No, Never
Welfare benefits	Yes	No, Never
Freebies	Yes	No, Never
Anchor babies	Yes	No, stipends to depart
Employer fees/fines	No	Yes -if one illegal employee
Reunification	33M in 10yrs	Not for Resident Visa Holders
Coerced-deportation	None	As needed for violations
Return to home country	No	Yes, with stipend
Must have healthcare	No	Yes
Must be employed	No	Yes
Must speak English in 2 yrs?	No	Yes
Oath of allegiance	No	Yes, after 1 year
Cost/debt accountability	No	Yes
Taxpayer Costs	$ 6Trillion	Zero
Payback plan	No	Yes
Accountability Database	No	Yes
Interloper fine	Yes	Yes
Employer fine	No	Yes (helps finance program)
Back taxes	No	Yes (vetting interviews)

Chapter 2 No Treat for Illegal Aliens Living in America

A Banana Republic President & Congress

There is no reason in this book to pine about a do-nothing Congress and a past president for over eight years who did everything to hurt US regarding the stain of illegal immigration on our shores. We have a solution without them.

In many ways, the effect on illegal foreign nationals in the US was as devastating and culturally almost as much of a shock as poor Africans being stolen to come to America to be placed in servitude. Think about it. The last eight years were not good years in American History. They were not good for foreign interlopers and they were not good for American citizens.

Congress either by action or by inaction permitted this travesty on the most vulnerable and most hopeful people on earth. Who knows what the African profiteers told the ultimate American slaves as they were forced to get on the ships to America. There are too many similarities. And, it is sickening on both accounts.

Greed in both cases was the cause. In these recent past years, US officials created a scourge on the illegal foreign national population. They did their jobs by working for barely enough to survive but greed again caused the new age robber barons to exact even a greater toll from their subjects. Illegal foreign nationals often replaced unknowing good-hearted Americans who had no idea what hit them.

Next thing they knew they were out of work or they were forced in order to survive to work under the table for peanuts. How could anybody knowing the pain so many people experienced want more of this in our country? Why does nobody with a powerful hand really want to solve this. Shame on politicians!

For Americans, our treasury is being depleted to feed foreigners while many Americans cannot find proper work to feed themselves. Perhaps it appears selfish while others too, from various countries are suffering, to focus on the treasury drain but this problem exudes a puss from the greed of the new robber barons that cannot be fought in normal means. The people's own representatives are against the people. This can be fixed but not by timid people. Americans must toughen up again like at our founding.

There are a number of countries who have a habit of exporting their poor to America because their greed causes them to find a sucker to permit them to have another layer on their cakes and another inch on their steaks, and more presents for their children than they can reasonably open in a day. "Ship the poor to America as those American dummies will put their own people in chains to give us even more profits." Plus, we will never have to look at those wretched half-people ever again. Drink up to the master's health! Drink Up1 Enjoy! If it is not that bad, at times, it sure seems like it is.

Figures available in 2012 show the immigrant mix from many areas across the world: 52% were from Mexico, 15% from Central America, 12% from Asia, 6% from South America, 5% from the Caribbean, and another 5% from Europe and Canada. Of course, it is right and proper for Americans to decide not to be chumps for these areas of the world. We don't even get help from our leaders. There are way too many traitorous American representatives asking us to turn our backs on their greed.

Stop the Treasury Drain!

The best way to stop the treasury drain is to send all the treasury sucking politicians back home. We must stand up and no longer take it just like we stood up and threw out lousy candidates for president. We are now forced to replace the Congress in order to do the right thing for America.

If a resident illegal foreign national really does not want to go home regardless of the incentive, then under the proposed plan, there is another option that actually costs taxpayers nothing and permits the interloper to stay in America indefinitely in a legal state as long as they "behave." Our greedy Congress more than likely will not like this either as it will result in higher wages which is unlikely to please political donors. Let's not let them stop us. Instead, we must identify them by their resistance so we can deliver their walking papers.

Americans are willing to help these poor souls who a corrupt Congress brought in to please their donors. But Congress may not want to help. The program provides for granting interlopers in good standing a *Resident Visa*. This is a new visa type that, unlike other visa types can be renewed each year. With this visa, former foreign nationals would be legal under the protection of the Resident Visa and could remain in America as long as they behave in a lawful manner according to the exact terms of their visa.

There are many differences between illegally gaining benefits in the United States and becoming legal by gaining a Resident Visa. Those choosing to employ the Resident Visa to stay in America, are welcome to do so; but the terms of the relationship with US officials will not be the same as when they were in illegal status. For example, there will be no more cash incentives.

For those very familiar with the notion of American visas, this unique visa permits those approved to live in America as long as they want and as long as they renew their Resident visa each and every year. In essence, this process provides a Resident Visa, an official US visa, which provides all of the benefits of a US non-immigrant category visa and more.

The liberal progressive ideology has a habit of taking words and making their usage appear to be, for want of a better word, *bad*. There is nothing intrinsically wrong with the word *illegal*, and there is nothing intrinsically wrong with the word, *alien*.

Moreover, when the term illegal alien, as used in US immigration law, is used in everyday speech, there is nothing implied that makes the term disrespectful to the person who fits the description. It is merely a statement of fact that permits an individual to be identified and described with accuracy without caring about their name.

What is meant by the term illegal alien

1. a foreigner who has entered or resides in a country unlawfully or without the country's authorization.
2. a foreigner who enters the U.S. without an entry or immigrant visa, especially a person who crosses the border by avoiding inspection or who overstays the period of time allowed as a visitor, tourist, or businessperson.

I hope nobody is upset by these facts as used by US immigration authorities for the very first laws on immigration.

Illegal alien, *illegal*, *undocumented*, and *unauthorized* are various labels used to describe people who have chosen to unlawfully reside in the United States, whether because of a clandestine border crossing, visa deadline violation, or other means. But these terms as defined by liberal progressives are not interchangeable. Each has a unique origin and connotation.

Alien for example, is a term used in legal language for a noncitizen resident, regardless of whether that person resides in the country legally or illegally. The term in the United States is inherited from British law, and has had a legal designation for foreign-born residents since the Revolutionary era. While the term continues to be used by the Department of Homeland Security and the United States Immigration and Customs Enforcement as a technical term in legal documents, leftists (progressive liberals) in America have made the term volatile and for their discourse it is not preferred. However, non-leftists find the term perfectly OK.

Though the terms *illegal immigrant* and *illegal resident* may have an anti-immigration connotation to leftists with an anti-American agenda, it is still largely accepted as proper.

The left likes to rework words for their own purposes and they are all about feeling good rather than fact. They do not care if Americans feel good but they go out of their way so that illegal aliens feel really good and are not offended by being called what they legally are: *illegal aliens*. To the left it is more sensitive to use the convoluted terms undocumented or unauthorized when describing these people, but this is not technically all that illegal and alien mean.

US immigration law uses the term illegal alien and does not waiver. The left has gone berserk in wordsmithing perfectly acceptable clear meaning words into unclear agenda-perfect words. Sometimes people actually get fired for not using the correct word or phrase. The left operates a dangerous game with words that only avowed leftists can fully comprehend. So, every now and then, an innocent gets fired.

Academic institutions have become subversive

The extremely subversive and politically correct Rutgers University student newspaper, for example, the Daily Targum, fired columnist Aviv Khavich , a Presidential Scholar, for trying to use the term "illegal alien" in a column about illegal immigration. So, as noted, it can be dangerous to not follow the prescription of the left but it does not make them correct. OK, as much as they hate the meaning of the words, it does not make them right.

After Khavich complained to his editor that she had changed illegal alien" to "undocumented immigrant" in the column in question which he acknowledges submitting, he was fired. Gone!. He was taken out by the politically correct Rutgers University Word Police.

Most of us know that "undocumented immigrant" is the term created by the Left and pushed by activist liberal organizations such as La Raza to obscure the illegal actions and conduct of those who violate our immigration laws. Khavich blamed the editor-in-chief of the student newspaper, Dan Corey, who claimed that "illegal" was changed to "undocumented" for "stylistic purposes." Corey apparently doesn't care that the Daily Targum's "stylistic change" is a refusal to use accurate legal terminology, which one would assume should be the goal of all news organizations.

Federal district court Judge Andrew Hanen of the Southern District of Texas dealt with this specific issue when he issued a preliminary injunction on Feb. 16, 2015. This judgement was against President

Barack Obama's immigration amnesty plan. This was in U.S. v. Texas, the lawsuit filed by 26 states to stop the "Deferred Action for Parents of Americans and Lawful Permanent Residents" program announced by Obama in November 2014.

This case went all the way to the U.S. Supreme Court after the Fifth Circuit Court of Appeals upheld the injunction. The justices split four-to-four on the case, leaving the injunction in place and the president's plan dead for the rest of his term. Leftists won't say this but "Obama lost the case."

Since we are suggesting that Congress create a brand-new visa category—Resident Visa--one might get the idea that there are thousands of US visa categories and that I am suggesting just one more. Not true! There are only two visa types today, and there will be just three three when the Resident Visa is fully described and approved.

What types of visas are there?

As discussed in Chapter1, the type of visa that a visitor or traveler must obtain is defined by U.S. immigration law, and relates to the purpose of the travel. There is one new category of visa proposed for current illegal alien US residents in addition to the two main categories of existing U.S. visas:

1. **Nonimmigrant visas**– For travel to the United States on a temporary basis.
2. **Immigrant visas**–For travel to live permanently in the United States.
3. **Resident visas**–New-- For current resident aliens to live temporarily in the US on an annually renewable basis.

Description of the new visa category

Under the new Resident Visa Program, a third type of visa will be authorized by US officials. It is called a Resident Visa. Current law says all visa holders must first have passports containing information such as their home country and other pertinent information. As other visas, the new visa category will also require a pre-existing passport.

The new visa category is intended for those residents formerly in an illegal status who register for and are granted a Resident Visa. Unlike other visas, the Resident Visa may be renewed annually as long as the holder does not violate the terms of the visa.

Like all visa requests, the individual must first possess a passport and then apply for the Resident Visa. The costs for the resident passport and the Resident Visa would be the same as under current law. An additional charge may be added to the visa fee for an ID card so the Resident Visa holder does not have to keep the passport and visa on their person at all times.

The visa is renewable annually for a $100 fee to reflect changes such as address or marital status etc. The ID card and photo and changeable biometric scans, if any, must be refreshed every five years.

Since the new program in its entirety, would provide for the voluntary egress of illegal aliens as well as Resident Visas for those who choose to stay in America, this is a combination plan. An interloper would get to execute just one of the two options. The name of the formal program reflects both options: *Stipend Return / Resident Visa Program (SR/RV).*

The part of this plan that most Americans will want to learn more about to assure that they are getting a fair shake is the Resident Visa Program. The Stipend Return Plan is fairly self-explanatory. My opinion is that it will remain the quiet part of this revolutionary program. Despite its serendipitous presence, it will save the US the most treasury tax dollars.

Years ago, a friend of mine told me about an experience he had with an IBM Executive that proved to him that business deals were like a marriage. *Both parties must bring something desirable to the table.* The SR/RV program is such a deal.

At the end of the day, the United States will have no more resident aliens. Can you imagine how positive that will be for all Americans and former interlopers alike. Instead, the former foreign interlopers will either have gained a Resident Visa and be legalized and be under the terms of the visa or they will be in their home countries cashing their massive stipend checks while preparing to knock them dead as entrepreneurs in their home countries.

No treat for illegal interlopers to live in America

Liberal progressives are kidding themselves when they think they are helping illegal aliens remain in this country. For most, living in the shadows and earning sub-minimum wages is like living in a hell-hole, hidden from the rest of America. When an interloper leaves the safety of the shadows today, their hearts beat ten beats faster.

Everybody knows that illegal aliens live as residents in the shadows, fearful of being seen by authorities for the continual fear of deportation. The shadows are America's poorest neighborhoods. Often, they are forced to live in abject squalor. Worse than that, they are treated as sewer-rats by the government and the liberal do-gooders who encourage them to come to America, promising them the world, while caring only for their votes. How do-gooders can feel good after delivering excrement sandwiches to these hard luck souls is a puzzle for many.

The businesses for which illegal foreign nationals work use the nastiest forms of labor arbitrage to trick the interlopers into working for slave wages without complaining. Nobody is saying slavery is or was ever good. However, it is undeniable that the slaves were fed, if for no other reason than to keep them strong and healthy so their output would be optimal. Today's illegal aliens are on their own and they have a hard time finding enough wages to be able to eat enough to live. It is no treat living in the shadows of America.

Anybody thinking that illegal aliens are having a daily picnic on American taxpayer expense are way off the mark for what is really happening. I say this without denying that supporting the meager existence of 60 million illegal interlopers requires quite a bit if US resources.

Big Business knows what it is doing. It has a great deal paying scant wages for top work. It is cheating American laws and American citizens by hiring illegal foreign nationals to get their work done on the cheap. They often do not pay even the minimum wage and they never pay the prevailing wage. If they paid the prevailing wage, think about it; they would not demand that the US Chamber of Commerce threaten Republicans into voting for amnesty.

American citizens are not attracted to such low-wage jobs; but worse than that, illegal foreign nationals are lured from their home countries thinking they are going to a better life. They quickly find that the big fat cats get the benefit of their labor without paying them a fair wage.

In his or her heart, the illegal foreign national worker knows they are in America illegally. They will do almost anything to not be discovered by others or turned in by their employers if they fail to produce. They live in the shadows with others of their ilk and they accept their plight because their only other choice is to leave the country to conditions that are perhaps even worse.

They know the dirty clandestine rules. And, so they accept wages that barely put food on their tables. Would fair-thinking Americans not be better off paying such victims stipends in their home countries rather than handing American fat cat businessmen the opportunity to exploit their labor and make their lives utterly miserable?

The US extends foreign aid in the amount of just over $50 Billion in total to countries who do far less for America than feed their citizens and make sure they have no need to come to America. We might do well to add $50 Billion to direct a national charity to help people in their home countries not require illegal passage to America to survive. Considering the current cost to America is about $500 Billion per year by not solving the foreign national crisis. Other estimates put the cost at One Trillion Dollars per year.

Paying to help people in their home countries is a far more charitable and economically beneficial idea. Why didn't Congress think of that? Could it be that it would not benefit their lobbyist's firms? Is our

Congress that corrupt? Who really wants to come to the Bronx, Scranton, PA, Podunk, IA, or Bloomfield NJ, when they can have a fine life in their home country

Americans are not really happy about the 60,000,000 illegals living in the shadows who the press says are not willing to even take a crack of assimilating in the US and melting into the melting pot. Why should we be? Yet, Americans do want illegal interlopers to be able to come out of the shadows and off the streets. I am one of them and that is why I wrote this book.

Many feel as I. At a minimum, we would like the destitute and hopeless who came illegally from foreign lands to come up out of the street gutters and at least get on the curbstones with the rest of us—who simply scrape for a living in these tough times.

We just don't want anybody, whether a foreign interloper or an American hard on their luck, looking for an easier life, to be able to get that life simply by sticking their hand in, let's say, my pocket. How would that be fair? What would that teach us?

Nobody who I know hates the illegal alien population but many Americans are well aware that the benefits that are accrued to dirty businesses are one way. They hire these poor souls and they exploit them for all they have. They take the best they have to offer while returning to them a mere pittance for their efforts. It is human greed over human goodness. Why don't reporters report the names of the people in business who hurt so many foreign nationals who want nothing more than a better life.

Let me be clear, however. The interlopers are half of the problem. If they did not crash our borders through physical travel of via Student Visa or H-1B visa or other visa over stays, this would not be the best-selling book that it is. Americans no longer want to be chumps. We'd love to help people in their home countries for $50 Billion a year rather than pay $500 Billion each year for taking care of them in America.

Wage impact

Unfortunately, Americans, born black or white, know that wages as a whole in America have gone down substantially as the scum of the entrepreneurial class have preferred to hire illegal foreign nationals as workers for slave wages to maximize profits rather than sharing a bit of their bounty with those who helped produce it.

In the meatpacking industry, for example, once dominated by unionized black workers—people who had worked their way out of poverty and well into the middle class over the years—once earned as much as $19.00 per hour in the 1980's. These victims of liberal interpretations of our immigration laws saw their average wages fall to just over $9.00 per hour as non-union illegal foreign national workers took over their jobs.

How did this happen. When companies moved from the big cities and built "worker cities," most regular Americans chose not to move. This action did not help black or white workers. If big business were honest about what happened, they would say that lowering the wages and hiring illegal workers did not help as the workers did not prosper as planned.

Case Farms, for example, built its business by recruiting immigrant workers, some of the world's most vulnerable, from Guatemala. They are forced to endure conditions, at times illegal conditions that few Americans would put up with. Big companies have gotten really bold in trying to squeeze out more profits on the backs of hard-luck immigrants whose wages keep going down.

Tyson Foods Inc., the nation's largest meat producer and processor, was indicted way back in 2001 with six employees on charges that it conspired to smuggle illegal immigrants across the Mexican border to work in its processing plants. How many do you think were successful? Big Business and the Democratic Party love illegal residents.

Simply leaving their home countries and coming to America adds little gold to the purses of the new immigrants. There are no free lunches even if when they appear to be free.

American citizens have been played for chumps by the big business tycoons and the vote-seeking dirty politicians in the progressive Democratic Party. If there was enough for everybody, Americans would not be complaining. While the average wage has been going down, big business, backed by the US Chamber of Congress have put America through the same labor arbitrage as when the Robber Barons chose to take it all at the end of the 19th century when many Americans had to work most of a 24-hour day in order to feed their families.

Americans do not want to hear the words *family reunification* ever again. The best place for family reunification for illegal aliens is in their home country. It is tough enough to absorb the illegal aliens themselves into the US welfare state with free education, free healthcare, and free this and free that. At the same times, daughters and sons of Americans are not as fortunate in the welfare game, simply because they are not illegal aliens.

American big shots on the charity scene seem to want to help those here illegally, but they have disdain for American citizens. They do not have the same charitable instincts to help John and Jane Doe of Regular America. Americans do not want charity. That is a fact. However, we do not want our taxes to pay for others who should have to work as hard as we do to survive.

Nobody wants to be a sucker and nobody wants to be a chump but corrupt American politicians have no problem dealing from the bottom of the deck for regular Americans.

Liberal progressives are always more generous with other people's dollars then their own. To know what I mean, check to see how much big millionaire liberals such as Al Gore give to charity. Just take a look in your own wallet and ask how much you personally are willing to contribute from your weekly salary to help say a mom and a baby living in America, so they can be reunited with a dad coming from the home country?

Knowing the mom came to America with her baby and she was fully aware that they would cause family separation does not engender a compelling feeling for any American to contribute to solve the problem. How much are you willing to contribute? When was the last time you sent a cash or check? Yet somehow it is easy if government takes from Americans and gives dollars in cash and services to illegal foreign nationals.

Here is another scenario. "Would anybody want to create trauma on a new illegal alien family by forcing them to make a go of it in America with no benefits from the government?" Nobody would want to hurt this family unless they were asked to pay the freight from their own wallets or personal savings.

The point is that there are many Americans, who have it tougher than those living in the shadows. Nobody is taking care of them. Jesus said, "the poor you will always have with you…" Illegal aliens must bear the consequences of their own migration decisions rather than asking US taxpayers to bail them out so they can live in America for free.

The Resident Visa program does solve the problem for Americans and illegal foreign nationals. A mom with a baby might cost taxpayers about $150,000 or perhaps much more over a five-year period. The Stipend-Assisted Return component of the immigration fix can be a great solution if the full stipend for two were $40,000 for example. In five years the US treasury would save $110,000 and the young family with a child citizen would have more than enough cash to go home to their own country and be reunited with all their family members, including the dad.

Since an anchor baby has many more rights as a citizen than a baby brought to the US, I would suggest a $50,000 stipend for anchor babies, no matter how old they may be. For a mom and a baby in that case, they would receive $70,000 in stipends. They then could start new lives with a nice nest-egg at home in their own home-town, not in the shadows of somebody else's town.

Add those who cross the border illegally to the visa over-stayers, and it is no wonder whole communities in the US are springing up in which over 90% of the residents are foreign interlopers. Since 1986 (to 2017 -- 32 years), the time of the massive Reagan amnesty, using the McCain rate of 4 million new illegal interlopers per year, the total number would amount to 4 X 32 = 128 million. That is an awful lot of people with many on the US welfare dole.

Should everybody come to America?

Some say that the US should have open borders? Ask them how much they are willing to contribute out of their own pockets when a human being is declared legal and citizen-like and thus able for the minimum $30,000 in benefits to which they immediately become entitled. I know the do-gooders' wallets are hidden by their accountants and regular American wallets are never fattened an iota, no matter how much we need, from any source—government or otherwise.

Yet, the illegal community gets bonanzas regularly from politicians, hoping one day to get their vote and from a Congress that hopes their actions will please the donor class to assure their reelections. Political corruption is now the law, not the exception in America.

Out of the almost 7 Billion in the world, there are approximately 3 Billion people, who are for their own reasons, not too pleased with their home countries. Low-ball estimates suggest that of these 3 Billion, there are from 500,000,000 to 1,000,000,000 ready to come to America immediately, as soon as we open our borders, and more would surely follow.

With 325 million people residing in the US today, and already most not able to find a parking space, let alone a job, can you imagine how crowded it would be if the whole world were to choose to relocate to the US.

To what country would the US be able to go to in order to get some financial relief so we would be able to afford the equipment and personnel to bulldoze government lands and our national parks to so we can build all the tent cities necessary to house the portion of the 3 Billion who would come to the US tomorrow if they could.

If they come, can we be assured that all of the citizens of the world will behave well? So far, no other country has been motivated to step up to help us if the world decides to relocate to America. Unlike the decisions of our Congress, the concerns of leaders in other countries is apparently for their own citizens.

The solution in this book that is concurrently being sent to the US government, addresses the matter completely, effectively, and fairly. I am a Democrat but this solution is just as appropriate for Republicans, Independents, and others. It is the product of copious research and a lot of thinking. As noted previously, it is called Stipend Return / Resident Visa Program. I would suggest that it should be passed and implemented ASAP. The problem with 60 million illegal interlopers in residence in the US becomes solved instantly.

Americans are always first in this plan. Moreover, it is not a denigrating notion to future Resident Visa Holders, who like other types of visa holders, are not citizens but are guests of our country.

Guests are guests; not owners

When you have guests in your own home, you still control your property. You do not let your guests do whatever they want to your property and lord over your family in any way. They don't decide it's lobster and steak every night on you.

If a person with a Resident Visa plays by the rules, more than likely, they will be able to stay much longer than a single year. But, if they do not behave well, the master of the house will send them off into the darkness and not permit a renewal. Yes, that means deportation with our best wishes and either no stipend or an appropriate allocation.

Perfection is tough to achieve

"In order to form a more perfect union…," starts of the Constitution noting that they had tried other forms of creating the union of states but this attempt, known as the Constitution is closer to perfect than any others that had had been tried, such as The Articles of Confederation.

Many probably know that over the last ten years, I wrote five other books dealing with the topic of illegal immigration and the resultant problem of having millions of interlopers as residents in the United States. The book titles are as follows:

- ✓ Taxation Without Representation
- ✓ Americans Need Not Apply
- ✓ No Amnesty! No Way!
- ✓ The Lifetime Guest Plan
- ✓ The Annual Guest Plan

This book is my sixth time trying to build a more perfect plan to deal with what today adds up to just about 60,000,000 uninvited visitors. Each time, as I wrote the next book, I created a better solution but it was not quite perfect. This time, with the Stipend Return / Resident Visa Program, it is my best effort yet. I am sure it is not perfect but it is more perfect than the Annual Guest Plan. I hope you think so also.

Though our immigration laws have been strong for a long time, it is obvious that our lax immigration enforcement over the last eight years created confusion as to the real meaning of our laws and it brought us the problem of people living in the shadows, and the problem is now clearly festering.

Both Democrat and Republican lawmakers lured illegal foreign nationals into our country to satisfy their own greed. The convinced interlopers that it was OK to come to America with no formal permission and no means of becoming a legal resident. That was wrong and it still is. Any solution today must consider America and Americans first; but it also must be fair to those who saw a real promise and went for it. The fact is that our corrupt politicians lied to the most vulnerable people in the world and the politicians gained from this deception.

One of the big problems in coming up with an acceptable solution is that political ideologies continue to clash over what is fair and right and acceptable. Some want outright legalization and citizenship while others want the letter of the law followed including mass deportations. The laws on the books are simply being ignored by public officials.

President Obama will be remembered as the biggest immigration lawbreaker of all-time. President Trump seems to be listening to what is needed somewhat but he too has put no solution on the table for the 60 million interlopers already residing in our cities. Building a wall is a great idea and it should be done but that is not going to solve the problem of having 60 million illegal residents costing taxpayers from $500 Billion to $1 Trillion per year..

The 60,000,000 solution

Over time, I kept researching and thinking and researching and thinking and finally it came to me. What if we made a deal with the interlopers and the American people that worked well for both? What if both constituencies, Americans and interlopers could agree to a real solution and be OK with it! Of course, our politicians would have to be convinced. After reading this book, you will be prepared that this is the solution and hopefully, you will do your part to help in the effort to make this plan into a reality.

I have already introduced the Stipend-Assisted Return / Resident Visa Program. There is a lot of goodness in this plan that makes Americans very pleased. The plan is good for Americans and it is a good deal for interlopers even if neither may see all the advantages at first. It should be the law of the land quickly and the problem with 60,000,000 shadow aliens in America is solved. Can you imagine. No more shadows? No more of a lot of bad things!

As long as the Resident Visa Holder is well behaved, and we Americans get to define what that means, they will have a right to live in America and hold a job for which an American citizen is not competing.

They may keep the jobs they already have. Resident Visa Holders will be 100% out of the shadows and will live like you and me within our neighborhoods, paying for housing and paying local taxes as we do.

Their kids will go to school and they will also pay school taxes like you and me.

In order to be approved for their status of Resident Visa Holder, they first obtain a special resident passport. They must promise not to be a burden (defined as costing taxpayers) or they will be asked to voluntarily return home. The government will help in their return home and in fact will offer substantial assistance of twenty thousand dollars or so for those who agree to go and not come back.

Americans will not pay a dime for Resident Visa Holders for social services such as education, healthcare or general living. The plan includes no free lunch, aka, no charity. Iron clad identification databases and ID cards with biometrics will be issued and those without such identification will be deported immediately once the program is in full force. With such a generous program available, there should be no reason why interlopers continue in the shadows.

By law, EMTALA emergency care must be provided to all residents, but these services are not intended to be free. A Resident Visa Holder who receives such benefits can make arrangements through the Accountability system (discussed in later chapters) to pay the fee for their services back to the US Treasury over an extended period if need be. They must not cost taxpayers a dime.

After an interloper in illegal alien status gains a passport from the Post Office or through any other acceptable government agency, they may then apply for their Resident Visa. The normal fee applies for a passport and for a visa as it always has for other visas. The Resident Visa fees will be the same or very similar to other visas. Any additional costs in this process other than the listed fees will also be borne by the interloper. The days of the free-lunch on American taxpayers are gone.

When the plan is in full force, it will include an Accountability System with a record for each interloper. This will establish a record and keep track of financial transactions paid for by the US government, and it will keep a running balance of how much each interloper owes America for the services they have taken from American Taxpayers. No cash payments shall be made although there may be reasons why a limited loan program might be instituted.

The amount to pay back for an interloper will include welfare and healthcare costs from over the years and anything else deemed by officials as items to be repaid. In addition to this accounting, those who cannot immediately pay fines and certain fees can have them added to their "account." Resident Visa Holders who work out a deal with officials to not be deported, will be expected to pay a small percentage of this account each year based on need, before their annual visa will be renewed.

A record of the stipends given to those participating in the Stipend-Assisted Return Program will also be accounted. Nothing provided to former interlopers is free. Everything is either paid immediately by the interloper or it is charged to the Accountability system in which reasonable payments will be expected.

To net it out, Resident Visa Holders can begin their freedom in the US tomorrow by getting a special passport at the usual cost. The one-time interloper will temporarily be deemed legal and will not be deported. Most Americans get their passports today at one of many Post Offices in the country and this passport procedure will either be the same or very similar.

When all illegal interlopers have their passports, US officials will know and will have records describing all of the former illegal foreign national residents in the country. Nobody will be hidden. This will have major value to our overall immigration enforcement efforts. At that point, an aspirant for the Resident Visa will become legal. They then must apply for the Resident Visa and be approved or agree to return home if they are not approved.

Those illegal interlopers who choose not to get a Resident Visa have the option of signing up for the Stipend-Assisted Return Program and will receive their return home expenses including transportation to their home country as well as a nice stipend by volunteering to return home through the program. They will not be permitted to return.

Americans believe the influx of illegal foreign nationals hurts them and from my own observations, we Americans are 100% correct. The table is turned in this program with American citizens now holding all the TRUMP cards.

To gain their Resident Visa status, they will agree to all the stipulations of the program such as to not vote in any election in the US for any office -- local, municipality, state, or federal. Unless they return to their home country, and begin a process like all others from that country, they can never become a citizen of the US.

Jumping the line is not permitted. However, if their home country, through its normal procedures in conjunction with the US Consular Office agrees to list them on their list for American Citizenship, after making the trip home, they will be able to return to the US using their Resident Visa.

There is no registration per se for the program. The program lasts for a year. An illegal interloper has just one year to acquire their specially designated passport. The passport cost the same as one for Americans traveling abroad. Once they have the passport, they are legal and they will be expected to apply for their Resident Visa within three months.

Most US non-immigration or worker visas are short in time scope, such as three to six months. The Resident Visa, however will be one year in duration and unlike other visas, it will be renewable annually. For the first five years of the program, the renewal will be in person and will cost $100.00. Every five years, the Resident Visa Holder will have their photo refreshed just as those re-applying for driver's licenses.

This Resident Visa is not to be thought of as a Guest Worker Visa, such as H-1B, as the recipient is not expected to be hired for any type of work under the auspices of the program. The key point here is that just like worker visas, the Resident Visa Holders are not citizens and they are not permanent residents. They not only can hold jobs, they must have a job in order to stay in good status. They are temporary visitors whose Visa type enables them to apply for renewal of their right of residence one year at a time. As residents only, they have no other rights such as those of today's green-card holder or US Citizen.

In essence, the Resident Visa provides these folks with an opportunity to be treated as visiting guests of American citizens. They are not American Citizens or ¼ citizens, or ½ citizens. They are simply guests and should not expect special treatment. Once approved, they have a special right granted by the citizens of the US to remain in the US as long as they are up-to-date on their Visa renewals and accountability repayments, are well-behaved.

Resident Visa Holders will have no special privileges. American Citizens have all the privileges of citizens in their own country / state, including first-option employment.

There are other advanced notions in the plan that may help US officials deal better with the ongoing issue of people wanting to crash into America uninvited for various purposes.

For example, The Resident Visa Program should never cost the US more than if the plan were not in force. Illegal foreign nationals who are granted a Resident Visa are not permitted to ever become a burden, financial or otherwise upon the citizenry of the USA.

In Chapter 1, you read a very light introduction to a very inclusive plan intended for the benefit of Americans. This Chapter adds detail to the description and subsequent chapters fine tune the program even further. Though the plan benefits Americans for sure, nonetheless it accommodates over 60,000,000 illegal foreign interlopers simply because America is a kind nation, and Americans have big hearts.

There is no reason for Americans to pay for visitors, wanted, or unwanted, though the burden for such interlopers has been very large for taxpayers for many years. The free lunch is over for all but those who choose to take a nice handout and return home from America and not return.

This is a much better deal than the Gang of 8

You may be aware that a group of Senators in 2013 created a monstrous anti-American solution to the same problem solved by the Resident Visa. They did not have a Stipend-Assisted Return in any part of their plan.

I took a hard look at this plan known as the Gang of Eight plan. I also looked at existing law, and other notions about how to solve the nation's problem with illegal residents. I found that none addressed all of the issues that having 60 million illegal foreign nationals in residence brought to America. When I read the Gang of Eight plan (Rubio, Schumer, Flake, and McCain) in 2013, it was easy to notice that it looked a lot like it was purposely designed to kill America. It did not solve the problem at hand.

With the Gang of Eight plan, no jobs would be left for Americans; newly unemployed Americans would have to pay for newly minted citizens; voting in national elections was not ruled out; 33 million more foreign nationals would be invited; It would cost over $6 Trillion.

It was a terrible deal for the country. I looked at all of the things that Americans did not like and then looked at what the illegal interlopers liked about living in America. I figured out a way to permit well-behaved interlopers to stay in America while giving Americans priority in all ways.

This plan which we have been discussing, The Stipend Return / Resident Visa Plan actually will work and it will solve the problem and take a huge financial burden off the backs of Americans. I rebuilt the plan and the rechristened the part for those wanting to stay in America as the *Resident Visa Program*. Those wanting to take a stipend and go home are welcome to use the *Stipend Return* Program. I think you're going to like this comprehensive solution. We take another look at how this compares with the Gang of Eight plan in a later chapter.

Chapter 3 A Nation of Immigrants

Columbus got us into immigration

Though the early immigrants mostly came legally, it is true from day one, those who call the United States a Nation of Immigrants have a just case. From its earliest days, America has been a nation of immigrants, starting with its original inhabitants, who crossed the land bridge connecting Asia and North America tens of thousands of years ago.

After Columbus, by the 1500s, the first Europeans, led by the Spanish and French, had begun establishing settlements in what would become the United States. In 1607, the English founded their first permanent settlement in present-day America at Jamestown in the Virginia Colony. There were many reasons why immigrants came to love in America but the bottom line has always been opportunity.

In his book, *A Nation of Immigrants*, John F. Kennedy writes, "There were probably as many reasons for coming to America as there were people who came. It was a highly individual decision."

The practice of one member of a family going to America first and then saving more funds to bring the others over was common. Though there were sporadic incidents of border crashing through ports, and across the borders, by and large US immigration was orderly and legal.

From 1900 to 1910, for example, almost 95 percent of the immigrants arriving at Ellis Island were joining either family or friends. Sometimes a parent, typically the father would come alone. He had a definite mission. It was to see if the streets really were paved with *gold*. It was his job to look for opportunities in the new world. When it was clear that coming to America it was a good deal, he would send for his wife and family.

Going back a little further to the mid 1900's, say from 1850 to 1910 the average cost of a steerage packet ticket (third class) was between $20 and $35. Tickets for 1st class at the time cost well above $100.00. Sailing time before steam-powered ships was about 21 to 30 days. As technological improvements were made, the typical time was reduced to about ten days. By the early 20th century (1907), the liner Mauretania with a capacity of 2,300 passengers was able to cross the Atlantic in 4.5 days, a record which was held for 30 years when the liner Queen Mary reduced the crossing time by half a day (4 days).

There were times in European and Irish history that landlords would pay the freight to get rid of poverty-stricken tenants from their properties and sometimes just to get them out of their country. They would buy the lowest cost ticket and help themselves rid the country of the poor, sickly, and destitute, while simultaneously helping, for example, the Irish immigrants especially during the potato famine. They'd get them on a sailing ship or perhaps a steamship to America and say, "good riddance." Speculation is that this was not an act of altruism.

Before American independence, The United States experienced major waves of immigration during the colonial era; the first part of the 19th century and from the 1880s to 1920. Many immigrants came to America seeking greater economic opportunity, but this was not the only reason. Most notably, the Pilgrims in the early 1600s, arrived in search of religious freedom.

From the 17th to 19th centuries, hundreds of thousands of African slaves came to America against their will. The first significant federal legislation restricting immigration was the 1882 Chinese Exclusion Act. The Federal government was mostly not involved in immigration enforcement until the later part of the 19th century.

Individual states regulated immigration prior to the 1892 opening of Ellis Island, the country's first federal immigration station. New laws in 1965 ended the quota system that favored European immigrants, and today, the majority of the country's immigrants hail from Asia and Latin America.

Between 1880 and 1930, over 27 million people found their way to the United States from various starting points around the world. Ocean liners were filled in both directions, as millions also returned to their home countries. A much smaller number of businesspeople and leisure travelers compared to immigrants crossed the oceans on steamships during this period.

It was tough to afford a trip to America as one would expect. Many immigrants sailed to America or back to their homelands in what were called packet ships. These vessels carried mail, cargo, and people. Most crossed the ocean in what was called the *steerage area*, below decks. It was also known as third class. Conditions varied from ship to ship, but steerage was normally crowded, dark, and damp. Limited sanitation and stormy seas often combined to make it dirty and foul-smelling, too. Rats, insects, and disease were common problems.

Illustrated London News, May 10, 1851 Courtesy of the Mariners' Museum

Ships took off from all over the world. From Liverpool, as an example, in addition to getting passage to America, travelers received the following:

"...each passenger receives weekly 5 lbs. of oatmeal, 2 1/2 lbs. biscuit, 1 lb. flour, 2 lbs. rice, 1/2 lb. sugar, 1/2 lb. molasses, and 2 ounces of tea. He is obliged to cook it the best way he can in cook shop 12 feet by 6! This is the cause of so many quarrels and...many a poor woman with her children can get but one meal done, and sometimes they get nothing warm for days and nights when a gale of wind is blowing and the sea is mountains high and breaking over the ship in all directions. —Anonymous, New-York Daily Times, October 15, 1851

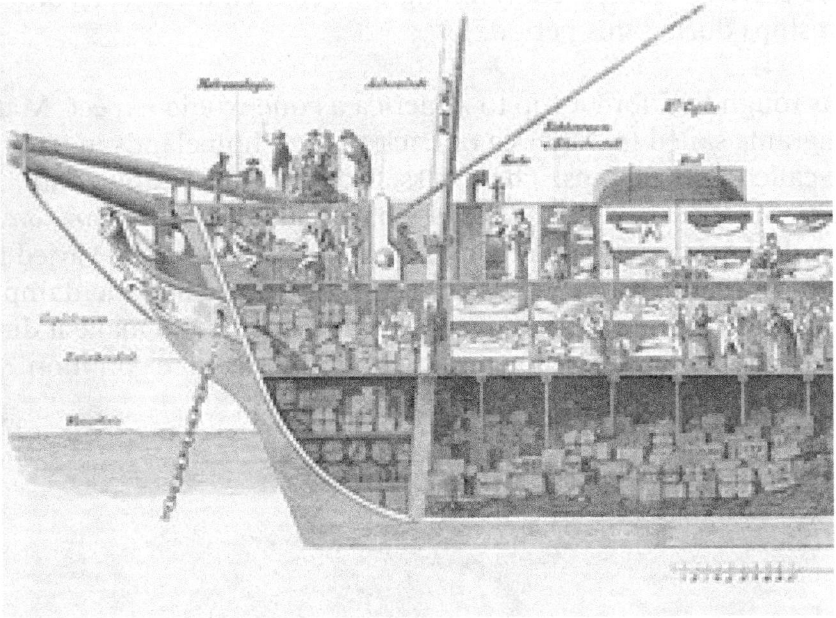

Inside a Packet Ship – Not much room

In 1903, when he was five, famous motion picture filmmaker Frank Capra (it's a Wonderful Life, et al.) emigrated to the United States with his family. They traveled in one of the steerage compartments of the steamship, Germania, which was the cheapest way to book passage. For Capra, the journey, which took 13 days on this particular ship, remained in his mind for the rest of his life as one of his worst experiences:

"You're all together – you have no privacy. You have a cot. Very few people have trunks or anything that takes up space. They have just what they can carry in their hands or in a bag. Nobody takes their clothes off. There's no ventilation, and it stinks like hell. They're all miserable. It's the most degrading place you could ever be."

""Oh, it was awful, awful. It seems to always be storming, raining like hell and very windy, with these big long rolling Atlantic waves.

Everybody was sick, vomiting. God, they were sick. And the poor kids were always crying."

With Capra's words, I think we can all feel the pain of the journey to America. But, once here, the new arrivals were thrilled.

Capra remembers the ship's arrival in New York Harbor, where he saw "a statue of a great lady, taller than a church steeple, holding a torch above the land we were about to enter". He recalls his father's exclamation at the sight:

"Ciccio, look! Look at that! That's the greatest light since the star of Bethlehem! That's the light of freedom! Remember that. Freedom."

In addition to second and third-class accommodations on the packet ship, a typical packet in the 1820s and 1830s could also accommodate 10 to 20 well-to-do cabin passengers. Rich or poor, many travelers alternated between anxiety and boredom on long ocean crossings, depending on the weather. For the more well-to-do, there was a saloon on the ship for libations.

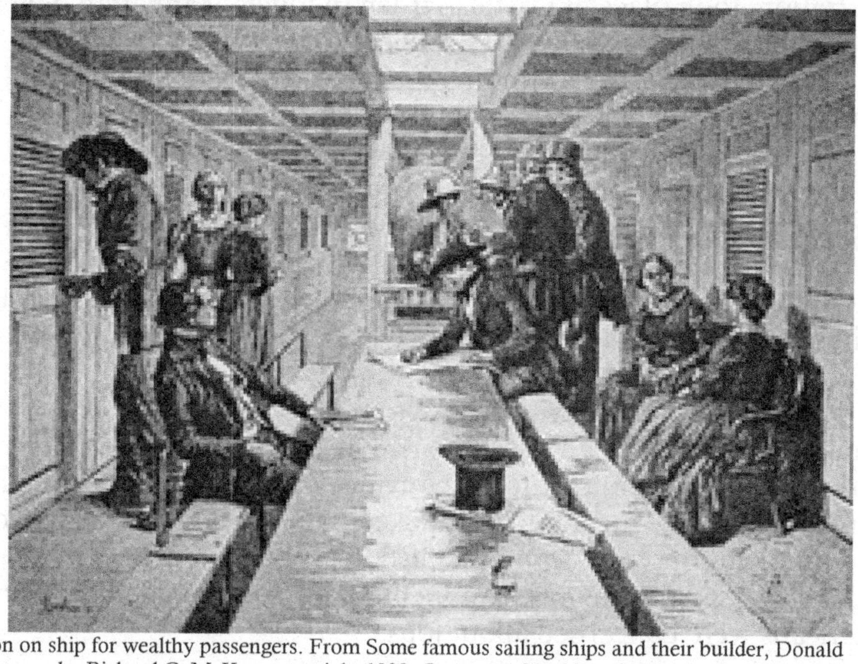

Saloon on ship for wealthy passengers. From Some famous sailing ships and their builder, Donald McKay . . . by Richard C. McKay, copyright 1928..Courtesy of Smithsonian Institution Libraries

Ellis Island – Feds took over immigration

When people today refer to Ellis Island, they generally speak about its major legacy in the national saga of immigration to America, standing with the Statue of Liberty in New York Harbor as a beacon of opportunity for the world's dispossessed. However, the building of a federal facility at the site of an old naval arsenal on Ellis Island in 1892 grew out of the newly established federal authority to regulate and restrict immigration.

Before immigrant processing was institutionalized by the federal government, at Ellis Island, states had the right to set the criteria for the suitability of immigrants, with an interest in recruiting labor and excluding potential wards of the state.

Two-thirds of the migrants to the United States between 1786 and 1892 came through New York City, and after 1855 immigration processing, including medical exams, customs inspection, and name registration, took place at Castle Garden in lower Manhattan, where social reformers set up voluntary services to help immigrants find work and housing. Similar immigration stations were located in Boston, Baltimore, and Galveston.

With the emergence of a vibrant US economy and a national transportation system in the years following the Civil War (1861–1865), immigration fell increasingly under federal authority as the national government was concerned about keeping America desirable for its citizens.

The federal government passed laws to restrict the entry of immigrants thought to be undesirable. For example, early efforts restricted the entry of prostitutes, convicts, incapacitated people, and contract labor. The most important exception to general practices of open immigration was Chinese exclusion. With so much Chinese labor being used for the transcontinental railroad and its many spurs, Americans were concerned about jobs.

And, so Chinese were singled out and the concerns about their labor activities was codified in federal law as the Chinese Exclusion Act of 1882. It established the prerogative of the federal government to raise restrictive barriers against specific national groups and to mark them as permanently foreign, aliens without rights. The situation with Americans complaining to the government about foreigners taking American jobs had gotten the attention of the Congress as you might expect.

Between 1880 and 1900, the pace of immigration to the United States had increased dramatically, with nine million immigrants arriving in these years. Laborers from England, Ireland, Germany, and the Scandinavian countries were now joined by new arrivals from Italy, Austria-Hungary, Russia, Canada, Greece, Syria, the West Indies, Mexico, and Japan. Nativists, especially those without jobs, were concerned that the new immigrants were taking away from America and this led to escalating pressures for a federal immigration policy.

This is not at all unusual in many countries of the world. The US was not the first to have concerns for its citizen population. Opposition to immigration commonly arises in many countries because of issues of national, cultural, and religious identity. The phenomenon has been studied in many countries such as England and Australia, as well as the U.S.A. and Europe.

Nativism has become a general term for "opposition to immigration." based on fears that the immigrants will distort or spoil existing cultural values. Sometimes it is valid and sometimes it is a pretext for misdeeds. There are sometimes situations in which the arriving immigrants greatly outnumber the original inhabitants, creating a deep fear in the citizens. In these cases, such nativist movements can help permit cultural survival.

The claim that immigrants can "swamp" a local population is related to birth rate relative to nationals. Contemporary opponents of immigration properly blame it for such problems as unemployment, crime (especially through gangs), harm to the environment, housing shortage, and overwhelming social services such as hospitals and safety such as police and fire protection.

Every new restriction generated more unauthorized immigration

There were various laws passed, the intention of which were to protect the existing American population from being overwhelmed. There were certain tests enabled as necessary to assure only the best came to America. And, so, new arrivals were required to pass literacy tests, pay what was called the head tax, or enter the country as one of a select few through the quota system in order to get one of the precious "slots."

As certain populations began to increase rapidly, laws were passed to specifically keep out Asians and Eastern and Southern Europeans, immigrants from those countries—as well as the others noted above. With the new restrictions, more and more "illegal aliens" began to enter outside of the legal system.

By 1925, the Immigration Service reported that over 1.4 million immigrants were living in the country illegally. Today that number is closer to 60 million. The New York Times, an honest news broker in the "Grey Lady" days, in a June 17, 1923 article, reported that W. H. Husband, Commissioner General of Immigration, had been trying for two years "to stem the flow of immigrants from central and southern Europe, Africa and Asia. They had been leaking across the borders of Mexico and Canada and through the ports of the east and west coasts."

Another Times article from September 16, 1927, described government plans for stepped-up Coast Guard patrols because thousands of Chinese, Japanese, Greeks, Russians, and Italians were landing in Cuba and then hiring smugglers to take them to the United States. Many immigrants were also violating the laws of their home countries, which required them to get permission to migrate, complete military service, or pay off debts prior to leaving.

Many European immigrants benefited from so-called "amnesties."

Acknowledging the large numbers of Europeans in the United States without proper authorization, the government devised ways for them to remain in the country legally. The 1929 Registry Act allowed "honest law-abiding alien[s] who may be in the country under some merely technical irregularity" to register as permanent residents for a fee of $20 if they could prove they had lived in the country since 1921 and were of "good moral character."

If there were just over 1 million in the country today, a Registry Act might do the trick but there would need to be additional restrictions. For example, more than 50% of green card residents in the US collect welfare and cash payments. Sixty-million new welfare recipients with Medicaid assistance would bankrupt the country. Look at the small numbers effected by the 1929 Registry act.

Roughly 115,000 immigrants registered between 1930 and 1940—80% were European or Canadian. Between 1925 and 1965, 200,000 unauthorized Europeans legalized their status through the Registry Act, through "pre-examination"—a process that allowed them to leave the United States voluntarily and re-enter legally with a visa (a "touch-back" program), or through discretionary rules that allowed immigration officials to suspend deportations in "meritorious" cases.

In the 1940s and 1950s, several thousand deportations a year were suspended; approximately 73% of those who benefited were Europeans (mostly Germans and Italians). With 60 million interlopers, even just 11 million as the liberal progressives preach, the US would be overwhelmed.

Instead what we have devised as a solution in this book is very simple to understand because the people affected already live in the US. Each requires a passport and a new type of visa called a Resident Visa. The restrictions attached to this Visa for those wanting legal status in this country protect the US from bankruptcy as the estimated cost of the new program to taxpayers is zero dollars.

Chapter 4 20th Century Americans Loved America

Early 20th Century Syrian immigration -- persecution

This next section is a story of my personal experience with Syrian immigrants who came legally to the US in the early 20th century.

My best friend in life when I was five years old was William. He is Syrian 100%. I am Irish 100%. Neither of us knew what we were and neither cared. I eventually learned that as one of two Irish families in a Syrian street block that the Irish were the minorities—at least where I lived. We sure never felt like it. William and I were simply 5-year old buddies and we loved each other's company and if it were OK to say then, we loved each other as human beings.

One full side of a double block separated our homes. George and Maryellen Sallitt lived in between us on the other side of our double. My family rented the half for $25.00 a month. We lived on the left side. The Sallitt side bordered William's property. Nobody cared who owned what from what I recall.

His family owned their own single-family home the next door down from the Sallitt's. It did not matter to William and me. By the way, I never knew and still do not know his last name. I don't know if he knew mine. It did not matter. We were buddies. There was a lot of trust between neighbors then and William and I trusted each other implicitly. It was implicit of course because neither of us knew what explicit meant.

I still do not know his dad's name or mom's but my older brother and sister played with his older siblings. Their names were unforgettable. Edna, Joheina, and Rudolph. What a nice family. My concentration was William and every day for me, in my neighborhood, from the time I knew that I was a human being, was a wonderful adventure. I never even knew my family and William's family were poor.

I am not sure if William enjoyed being in my house as much as I liked being in his house. In my house, it was peanut butter and jelly and white milk. In his house, it was a cavalcade of great smells and different smells every day. It took me a while to be convinced to try to taste some of the food behind the smells. The scent was both alluring and foreboding.

Would I die if I tried the food? I had reason for concern as I had a documented weak stomach. At my favorite cousin's home, Richard Knaus, I had tried my Aunt Helen McKeown's macaroni and beef and I threw up too quickly to be excused. So, I always walked fearfully back then when asked to try something made by anybody but my mom or grand-mom.

Grape leaves arranged to allure strangers to their magic.

Who knows? Have you ever smelled grape leaves coming out of the oven? Soon, the smells in William's home got to me and I told myself *no throwing up!* Once invited to the table, I could not get enough of the daily cacophony of items from grape leaves to kibbee to baklawa to whatever it may have been on a particular day. I began to trust my schnozzle and I knew finally that my best friend's family had no designs on killing me with great food. But they did love that an Irish kid two houses up loved it so much.

Once I got the hang of trusting that the smells would deliver great tastes, as a five-year-old, I was in. My mom and dad and grand-mom could keep the p b & j sandwiches. Yet William seemed to like them nonetheless. We remained the best buddies in life until he moved away unexpectedly and to this day, I have never seen him again.

But, I remember him like yesterday. I never thought deeply about stuff like that while a youngster, teenager, young adult, or an old fart as I find myself today. When I wake up and think of my buddy William, I ask myself, why can it not be like that today for everybody of different ethnicities?

Subsequently, I learned that the "William" family were originally refugees from Syria and like my great buddy George Elias who grew up with me post William on High Street in Wilkes-Barre, PA., they moved to America to avoid what was known as an Ottoman / Muslim persecution. They could have been killed or they could have come to America. They had two choices. These are things that if I had not asked my friends from High Street, I would have never known.

As a historical point of note, the Ottoman authorities looted, killed and deported Orthodox Syrians. In 1915–16, the number of Orthodox Syrians in the Diyarbakır province was reduced by 72%, in the Mardin province by 58%. They were serious times for sure—in many ways like today.

So, why is this little anecdote important in life?

It is because it is important in the lives of all Americans. This book is about illegal aliens from many different countries who have come to our country, by violating our laws. George and William—their families—came to America because they wanted to live and not die at the hands of those wanting to kill them in their home country.

William and George's families did not use gimmicks or tricks to jump the line to get to America sooner and become citizens sooner than their comrades in their home countries? No! They went through the American process as tough as it was to become not only a temporary resident in the great USA but also to go further and eventually become citizens. It was no picnic becoming a citizen but the work was worth the effort. Being a citizen of the United States is an honor and a privilege.

I met my friend William and my friend George after their families had gone through the arduous process of becoming Americans. They loved America. As sons of Americans, both of my friends when they were born, because their parents worked so hard to be Americans; were Americans at birth. Nothing in life worth having is easy!

Families like William's and George's no longer come legally.

What has changed? Today's illegal aliens for the most part decided to live in America, period. That's it. They did not want to do the work and get in line to come here legally. Their plan was to jump the line to get a job whether under or above the table. They know the job will pay more than $6.00 per day, which is what they make south of the border. It is no picnic getting to the US and hiding all their lives. I do not contest that.

Some are willing to endure mistreatment by coyote human smugglers, or go it alone, risking it all by enduring long journeys by foot, train, or boat. to make it across the border. Some from China and elsewhere get backing to come by airplane. But for an increasing number of immigrants, illegal status can arrive overnight, without a single step, because US enforcement of its visa laws is so lax.

In each year from 2007 to 2014, for example, more people joined the ranks of the illegal by remaining in the United States after their temporary visitor permits expired than by creeping across the Mexican border, according to a report by researchers at the Center for Migration Studies.

Illegal interlopers—a major cost—to taxpayers

Americans view most illegal alien residents as a cost burden in their lives. These unlawful residents take whatever they can get from the system, paid by American taxpayers. Sometimes even when they have jobs, they figure out how to get more from the public system.

Robert Rector, MA, Senior Research Fellow in Domestic Policy at the Heritage Foundation, and Jason Richwine, PhD, Senior Policy Analyst for the Center for Data Analysis at the Heritage Foundation (at the time of the quote) in their May 6, 2013 Heritage Foundation Special Report #133 on Immigration titled "The Fiscal Cost of Unlawful Immigrants and Amnesty to the U.S. Taxpayer," available at heritage.org, stated:

"In 2010, the average unlawful immigrant household received around $24,721 in government benefits and services while paying some $10,334 in taxes. [Since then over the past seven years at inflation rates, this number would be more like $30,000.] This generated an average annual fiscal deficit (benefits received minus taxes paid) of around $14,387 per household.

This cost had to be borne by U.S. taxpayers... Under current law, all unlawful immigrant households together have an aggregate annual deficit of around $54.5 Billion."

The $54.5 Billion figure is a very low estimate as it is based on a never changing 11 million illegal alien population residing in the country for the last twenty years.

Senator John McCain refutes these numbers. McCain says 4 million come each year illegally and that would make 128 million illegal interlopers since 1986, the last amnesty. 11 Million is a farcical number. My own estimate is about 60 million given that some go back and forth at will.

The Federation for American Immigration Reform (FAIR) wrote in its Feb. 2011 article "The Fiscal Burden of Illegal Immigration on United States Taxpayers" on fairus.org:

Using the 11 million number, "Illegal immigration costs U.S. taxpayers about $113 Billion a year at the federal, state and local level... The annual outlay that illegal aliens cost U.S. taxpayers is an average amount per native-headed household of $1,117... Education for the children of illegal aliens constitutes the single largest cost to taxpayers, at an annual price tag of nearly $52 Billion...

At the federal level, about one-third of outlays are matched by tax collections from illegal aliens. At the state and local level, an average of less than 5 percent of the public costs associated with illegal immigration is recouped through taxes collected from illegal aliens. Most illegal aliens do not pay income taxes. Among those who do, much of the revenues collected are refunded to the illegal aliens when they file tax returns...

With many state budgets in the red, policymakers have an obligation to look for ways to reduce the fiscal burden of illegal migration. California, faced a budget deficit of $14.4 Billion in 2010-2011, was hit with an estimated $21.8 Billion in annual expenditures on illegal aliens. New York's $6.8 Billion deficit is smaller than its $9.5 Billion in yearly illegal alien costs."

Both California and New York are in even worse shape today. Citizens from other states are now balking that the Federal Government (you and me) should not bail out either of these anti-American states that choose to treat aliens better than citizens. .

Considering that all of these estimates used today find 11 million Billion illegal interlopers as their basis, it is more proper to use cost projections based on John McCain's estimate of 128 million illegal residents in 2017 or my well-researched estimate of 60 million as used in this book. Using the proper basis, all of a sudden, the annual cost goes from $100 Billion per year to either $500 Billion if you use my estimate or $1000 Billion ($1 Trillion), if you use Maverick McCain's.

The bottom line of course is that such unchecked migration is a major financial burden on US citizens no matter how it is sugar coated. The US is $20 Trillion in debt. One can say that with a $1 Trillion per year burden that it would take just 20 years to hit $20 Trillion. That is a big burden attributable to countries that choose to export their poor. America has a right to protect its self-interests.

Study by Center for Immigration Studies

Steven A. Camarota, research director at the Center for Immigration Studies, crunched the numbers and he found that the current population of illegal immigrants (using the popular number 11 million) will drain nearly $750 Billion from taxpayers over their lifetimes — amounting to six times what the deportation costs would be. Yet, liberals will tell you we cannot afford deportation. Actually, we cannot afford to feed and nurture a population of foreigners who are in this country illegally.

If the US were your business, you would want to figure a way out of this fiscal mess. Our Congress seems happy to let it continue so they get the votes and / or business gets employees for slave wages. A Congress that thinks this way must be replaced.

When families are brought in by our generous reunification provisions, the costs are actually higher as the new migrants are legal and they take advantage of every welfare program that our clever Congress has designed. Here are some facts about legal immigrants from a recent report by CIS. Many of our current immigrants come from what began as an illegal migration and then they anchor a child with an American birth. In all cases, the US taxpayer pays a huge toll for the new legal immigrants.

We know that we cannot afford illegal aliens but another valid question is: "Can we afford legal immigration—especially that based on the huge family reunification umbrella. Almost everybody is related to somebody and we have no means of verification?"

1. An estimated 49 percent of households headed by legal immigrants used one or more welfare programs in 2012, compared to 30 percent of households headed by natives.
2. Households headed by legal immigrants have higher use rates than native households overall and for cash programs (14 percent vs. 10 percent), food programs (36 percent vs. 22 percent), and Medicaid (39 percent vs. 23 percent). Use of housing programs is similar.
3. Legal immigrant households account for three-quarters of all immigrant households accessing one or more welfare programs.
4. Less-educated legal immigrants make extensive use of every type of welfare program, including cash, food, Medicaid, and housing.
5. The overwhelming majority of illegal immigrants have modest levels of education; therefore, the high use of welfare associated with less-educated legal immigrants indicates that legalization would likely increase welfare costs, particularly for cash and housing programs.
6. Restrictions on new legal immigrants' access to welfare have not prevented them from accessing programs at high rates because restrictions often apply to only a modest share of immigrants at any one time, some programs are not restricted, there are numerous exceptions and exemptions, and some provisions are entirely unenforced. Equally important, immigrants, including those illegally in the country, can receive welfare on behalf of their U.S.-born children.

If it were your house and your wallet, as kind as I am sure you are, I bet you would not be so generous that you give up your house and you empty your wallet.

Chapter 5 Illegal Immigration Erodes Equality

Legitimate immigration was necessary

Illegal immigration insidiously erodes equality under the law. Americans are all pro-immigration to the extent of our laws. If Americans were not pro-immigration for example, Columbus and his shipmates and their families more than likely would have withered away from disease or cold winters or they would have lost their battles with the Indians. Additionally, all fifty states; at least the mainland's forty-eight, would probably now have Indian derivative names, such as *Redskins*, and they would probably be run by the same financial wizards who run today's highly successful casinos.

After the USA was in operation as a country with a Constitution for just several years, its population was not much more than 4 or 5 million people. This is just a million or two more people than the annual flow of illegal immigrants from south of the border. This was of course before the illegal children (DACA) revolution brought to us in our time by our immediate past president and his unconstitutional DREAM executive orders, because Congress did not give him his way.

America is fortunate to have Senator John McCain as a self-recognized expert on illegal immigration, having authored several bills that attempted to force amnesty in the name of comprehensive immigration reform down the throats of American citizens. Senator McCain would never stretch the truth about his knowledge of illegal alien crossings per annum.

A supporter of unfettered immigration, the Senator would more than likely have maximized, not minimized the numbers crossing the border each year. McCain wanted everybody in the world to come on down and get a nice handout while you are at it.

Yet, in a letter dated February 2004, Senator McCain, recognized by many as one of the few valid authorities on the subject of immigration, noted that the flow of legal immigrants per year is in the millions and that the flow of illegal aliens, using 2002 as his base year of reference is approximately four million per year.

Though we rarely agree with the Senator from the great state of Arizona on anything, we agree with him on this. We also know his word is final in Democratic circles about important issues on the subject—such as the number of crossings per year. I did not write this letter for Senator McCain but I have been well aware of these huge numbers of annual crossings for some time.

McCain stated emphatically in his letter that Border Patrol apprehension figures demonstrated that "almost four million people crossed our borders illegally in 2002.Experts on the subject agree that illegal crossings have only increased since then until 2017 when under

President Trump's watch, they are down to 30% of the norm, which is still over 1 million crossings per year.

Our starting year for all counting is 1986 when President Reagan provided the last carte-blanch amnesty to all illegal aliens in the country. Many in other countries benefited as US enforcement was held back for this period.

If we were to add up the numbers from 1986 with President Reagan's amnesty and if we used John McCain's figure of 4 million per year for 32 years through 2017, the total in our country illegally today could be easily estimated at 32 X 4 = 128 million. It is an answer derived by McCain's numbers and a little multiplication for the 32-years of disregard for border protection. Yet, the press hides these numbers from US and for years, they have claimed the number is a constant 11 million.

My estimates from a more acute observation has the number much closer to 60 million than 11 million or 128 million. Either way, 128 million or 60 million—that is a big burden and a lot of dependents for American taxpayers to carry on our backs.

The biggest # I have seen admitted to by the biased press is 20 million. The press and the government lie to us so that the Mexification of the US can go on unfettered. When the illegals outvote citizens in local, state and national elections, it will already be too late.

The Founders were not kidding about immigration

History has recorded that on March 26, 1790, almost 225 years ago, the second session of the first Congress (operating under the Constitution with a real House and a real Senate) approved the new nation's initial effort to create the rules under which foreign-born persons could become U.S. citizens.

After these laws, from this point on, our borders were not open per se, and we had these laws (rules) for how those wishing to be Americans could come to visit or to become Americans. No American then and no American today ever would have agreed to a notion called permanent residents who merely wanted to hang on, pledge no allegiance, and take whatever benefits the welfare system would give them.

All Americans after the date of the first immigration law, who immigrated were to follow this new law of the land. The law that was put together in 1790 did not suggest as President Obama seemed to believe for the last eight years, that foreign interlopers should go ahead and violate the US law, step on US soil, and then not worry about hiding from US officials simply because the President would assure that nobody would bug them. The founders wanted America to remain pure with those who loved America in charge of America.

The Naturalization Act of 1790 was specific in what needed to happen for foreigners to become citizens. The law specified that "any alien, being a free white person," could apply for citizenship, so long as he or she lived in the United States for at least two years, and in the state where the application was filed for at least a year. The new law also provided that "children of citizens of the United States that may be born … out of the limits of the United States shall be considered as natural born citizens."

In effect, this law left out indentured servants, slaves, and women. Later Constitutional Amendments added all American constituents. The 1790 law also mandated that one must "absolutely and entirely renounce and abjure all allegiance and fidelity to every foreign Prince, Potentate, State or Sovereignty." In other words, the US demanded loyalty for its citizens or you would not make it. Nobody ever conceived of a permanent resident who was above US laws and yet who could pontificate about how the US conducted its business.

There was no diversity. There was a melting pot. If potential citizens did not want to melt in the melting pot with everybody else, they were expected to be excluded from living in America. Permanent visas were 10 year visas renewable but not intended to be permanent. Who would do that. If you want to be and American, become an American now that you are a green card holder. If not, get the h… out!

Though these terms were seen by the people at the time of the founders as quite generous, still the law denied the right to naturalize to "persons whose fathers have never been resident in the United States." Fair or not, this was the law of the US! It is not up to government employees, even if elected, to write their own laws.

Immigration law was becoming more important and the laws have been changed several times since 1790. For example, in 1795, as anti-immigrant feeling began to grow in the country the Congress responded to the people's concerns. The necessary period of residence to become a citizen was increased from two to five years. Immigration law became firmer as the nation aged. Americans wanted America to be America, not a suburb of a country that wanted to be independent of America's laws.

Enter special interests, who like to bypass laws and have their friendly "owned" politicians let them get away with it.

Regarding immigration, you already know that there are two major special interests. The first special interest is the Democratic Party, which believes that if all illegal foreign nationals were to be immediately made citizens, the Democrat Party would never lose another election. That is a great motivator for them to want to bring all foreigners in immediately and make them all citizens of this nation. The corrupt press has aligned itself with the causes of the Democratic Party.

And, so, even though illegal alien workers have taken American jobs and substantially driven down the average weekly wage, still your "friendly" Democratic Representatives in Congress advocate amnesty and citizenship for them, with no questions asked, even if they break our laws. Your Congress promises less prosperity for all American citizens to accommodate foreign nationals because this will help Democratic politicians continually get elected.

The Republicans have skin in the game also. The Party of Lincoln encouraged by donors, large and small businesses, and, the anti-US-employee US Chamber of Commerce, is 100% for keeping illegals safe from harm so that they will keep working for peanuts and bolstering business profits. They do not want anything like the Resident Visa Plan as proposed in this book because it would mean the former interlopers, who would become Resident Visa Card Holders would be working for higher wages, which would have to be paid by the Republican donors.

There was nobody working for American citizens before Donald Trump was elected. That, of course is one of the reasons that the Republican Swamp and the Democrat Swamp hate the new President.

Unfortunately, most Americans, have not been convinced yet of the theory that most of their representatives have become socialists and communists looking for a poor and continually underserved, very needy underclass. The idea is that this new subjugated group of illegal residents will be appreciative of dirty politicians and continually vote these dishonest knaves back into office at their own peril.

The major concern of corrupt politicians is to assure that the Democrat members of Congress get reelected and another Democrat president rets elected next time and every time. One can explain the fanaticism of the left regarding President Trump. They simply cannot handle that their marked deck was discovered by regular people and their corrupt candidate was rejected.

Nonetheless, that really is the most important concern of the Democratic Party and it is also a major concern of the Republican Party. In other words, American citizens do not even register on our representatives' radar—Democrat or Republican.

Bringing in poor, uneducated, people from south of the border, often criminals, who feed from our welfare system, taking tax dollars from those with minimal incomes, assures the Democratic politicians of the illegal's votes for a long time once they are in America. Who pays for these illegal aliens?

It is the working slobs such as you and I who happen to pay taxes, who pay for them. Of course, the poor guy who twenty-years ago was once making $19.00 an hour in a meatpacking job and now with no union protection from illegal workers, is forced to work for $9.00 per hour in the same job. That guy has paid for them for twenty years.

Americans, mostly black, who labored for the big wages in the meatpacking industry of yore, had a choice to work for $8.00 or $9.00 per hour if they did not complain. They did not have the option, however, to keep the $19.00 per hour wage that they had won in prior Union negotiations.

Their other choice was not to work in meatpacking. Nobody in government was protecting the American wage v the illegal foreign national wage. Nobody even talked about the fact that under the covers of the flag such nasty labor arbitrage with foreigners was occurring.

But, the US Chamber of Commerce was fully briefed that their business constituents could add hundreds of millions of dollars to their bottom lines simply by stiffing these poor know-nothing slobs from other countries who had come to America to pick gold in the streets. And, if regular Americans had to reduce their wages by 50% so these fat cats could easily grab these great profits, so be it!

My point ladies and gentlemen is that calling these poor souls lured into involuntary servitude in the US, illegal aliens or illegal foreign nationals showed the people of America that there was a problem. It brought out the problem of their being here. Having to change the nomenclature and not call them what they were meant that poor American slobs left in the dust by dirty politics would seem like they were whining if they complained that their families were suffering from illegals taking their jobs and working for less than the minimum wage.

It was and is a major conspiracy of the Democrats, Republicans and the national media who hate fairness for Americans. Their objective is that all Americans, rich and poor simply come to condone labor arbitrage and slave labor as an inevitability of life in America. Think about it. I don't buy it. And, I am pleased that President Donald Trump does not buy it either.

As long as the Republican Donors were pleased, Republican candidates would fight for sub minimum wages forever for illegals and would never try to get them deported or moved to a citizen class that permitted them to live out of the shadows and have a normal fear-free-life.

That my friends is the definition of national political corruption.

Illegal foreign nationals are simply tickled to get $8.00 or even less than the minimum wage even while knowing they are being exploited. The C of C knows that multiple ID's, which they seem to condone as a cost of the benefit of slave labor, the unaffected C of C thinks their gluttonous greed can be explained away that illegal foreign nationals are simply clever entrepreneurs who often collect unemployment and welfare while holding a job.

The C of C is a corrupt organization and that is why they should no longer matter to regular Americans. Who pays for the largesse of America's big business fraternity? You and me—that's who!

The second special interest (Republicans) as noted previously, are also on the take and against regular people. They do not ever gain at the ballot box. However, illegal foreign nationals do provide huge gains in the wallets of American business and the campaign coffers of dirty Republicans.

American businesses love paying the smallest wage possible and since illegal foreign nationals work for peanuts, there has been a perfect marriage of needs. The point is that both the leaders of the Democratic Party and the leaders of the Republican Party are fighting against American citizens (the voters) when they permit illegal aliens to live in America with impunity at the expense of American labor. But, their own needs come first and are best satisfied by their lobbyists and special interest friends. I wish it were not that way but it is.

Traditional Republican politicians have had great alliances with businesses for many years. They had once been directed by their Republican donors, representing big businesses and corporations, to ignore the pleas of constituents who are out of work.

Their job, in order to continue the flow of donations to their campaign chests, is to assure businesses a steady flow of illegal cheap labor. So far with no border fence, no border wall, and eight years of Obama-suspended border enforcement, both Democrats and Republicans have been well pleased with themselves.

For their work in tamping down and delegitimatizing American sentiment about illegal aliens; they get big campaign contributions. The only groups, who align with the majority of Americans and who oppose blanket amnesty and who are 100% pro-American citizens philosophically, are conservatives, nationalists and populists, such as those who once were members of ad-hoc TEA Parties.

Are TEA Parties bad?

If you get a wrenching feeling in your stomach when you read TEA Party, I can explain it for you. The press today is corrupt, period. They are also very corrupting. They make you think that lies are truths and that truths are lies. They want you to hate all things conservative and all things Trump and all things TEA Party. They are joined at the hip with the progressive liberal Democratic Party, and do not support the people per se.

The corrupt US media has de-sensitized many Americans to their bias. The US media in many ways is anti-American but they do not tell you that they are communists. They do not want you to know. They do not tell you that they do not give a damn whether you or your children do well in America.

Why? Well, they still want you to listen to them on the radio and TV and they want you to buy their newspapers and believe the slop they write. They know that if they tell you the truth, you won't like them much anymore.

So that you would not think it through by yourself, the media lied continually about the TEA Party right from the start. And, they lie about anything that hurts their progressive / socialist agenda and their backing of the Democratic Party. They do not deliver the real news to Americans yet most of US forgive them for their lack of honesty anyway.

Americans love to forgive people—even those laughing at them as they stick a sword in their heart. Since they all have big popular names, they think the small people like US will take their "bull" and believe it. That was then and folks, this is now.

Enough of the population did as prescribed in 2008 and again in 2012 to elect and reelect the first bona fide incompetent president. Yes, he is known as the first black president though he is half black and half white. I believe that his white side is incompetent and his black side is fully competent and actually pretty smart from my readings about his life. And, so, this is not a racist notion or an accusation. It is just an opinion based on the facts as I see them.

Unfortunately for America, former president Obama and his brood in the current deep state have not chosen yet to vacate fully their offices or virtual offices in the US government. After eight years, this residue still stains the offices of government workers in Washington and elsewhere.

As I read my facts in newspapers as did the former president, these sycophants of the former president, aka *the deep state*, are trying to tell us all that the new president is illegitimate. How do they know? Perhaps it is because he is not the old president but facts are used sparingly in their arguments. All I know is that this new guy in the Oval Office is the next best thing to Ronald Reagan and before that, it would be Jack Kennedy (JFK), another of my favorites.

If you are a hard and fast left-winger, the actions of the press may please you but if you simply love America, their actions should enrage you. We all need to know our rights to fight a dishonest press. Knowing that most of our rights stem from the Bill of Rights and the others directly from the Constitution means that we need to understand the contents of these bastions of freedom and liberty so that neither the deep state, nor other corrupt parts of government can have their way with US.

Conservatives differ on immigration with elitist Republicans, and opportunist Democrats. No American citizen, suffering from the worst economy since the depression would be asking the government to invite in more wage lowering workers. How does adding to the worker pool help American citizens get jobs?

Thomas J. Donahue, President of the US Chamber of Congress (C of C) is one of the most despicable men in America. Remember him and do not forgive him until he confesses. He is a man who knows what is right but chooses another course of action despite what he knows because he is owned by big business. Very powerful people in America control him and everything he does. Donahue is a nobody directed by money directed to usurp Americans who believe the C of C is representative of good Americans. When you as an American hear C of C, think of an organization that wants foreigners to overwhelm American labor.

Mr. Donahue had the gall to tell people in a major US Primary Election—I mean the Republican Presidential Candidates (many current lawmakers) when deciding what issues, they should be for or against that "if they do not pass amnesty, the Republicans shouldn't bother to run a candidate in 2016." How about that?

The C of C represents donors whose interpretations of the Constitution do not represent the real Constitution as noted by regular Americans. There are those of us who taught at Business Schools and who know the C of C is wrong but then again, the C of C is owned by those who want the best for them, not for America.

The big donors for the C of C are those who support all the bad guys who President Donald Trump refers to as *The Swamp*. Why Trump's leanings against corrupt money changers does not soften his detractors such as the C of C and others really does puzzle me. But, let's move on.

The C of C cares nothing about workers' salaries but it cares a lot about corporate profits for Republican donors. Donohue, who is not a favorite of regular Americans, expected Republican lawmaker members to pass a John McCain, Lyndsey Graham, Jeff Flake and Marco Rubio style amnesty (Gang of Eight) bill rather than forego campaign funding from the Chamber.

Our most noteworthy Republicans, including John McCain, Jeff Flake, Lyndsey Graham, and Marco Rubio sold out Americans for foreigners in this Senate-passed "almost-law." Thank God, we have a House of Representatives that face the people every two years in real elections or the anti-American immigration stuff that these four Republicans tried to throw at us in 2013/2014 might have stuck.

The US Senate, long controlled by Democrats, passed a global amnesty bill in early 2014. The goal was to nail Americans by giving their jobs to foreigners. Democrats do not like American citizens in need, if they do not want to accept government help.

The Democrats, of which I admit I am still one, pressured the House of Representatives to do the same as the Senate throughout 2014. The bill went down to a big defeat and our new President promises that all of the even breaks from now on will go to American citizens not illegal foreign national interlopers and big money.

In Obama-times, the conservatives in the House blocked a vote on the McCain amnesty package. Speaker Boehner, who could easily have been a Democrat and nobody would have known that he had switched, did not help the conservative cause. He was under pressure from regular people, because he appeared always ready to cave to the more powerful Obama and the Republican elite and the big ambidextrous donors in the C of C.

This vote eventually did take place in the House in 2014, and the coalition of the anti's—McCain, Flake, Graham, and Rubio lost but America won. The House did not go as the Senate did. Just this one time. The Gang of Eight Bill did not pass because Americans would not accept it.

As a Democrat with little allegiance to the D party platform, I think I scribe honestly about what I see. I do see the Democrats at least as being honest about wanting to kill America. I do not like the facts in their honesty but who can complain about honesty?

hat is surely one of the D objectives. They do not deny it so how can we fault them for their bravery and honesty about items on their agendas that will destroy America.

The Republican House was ambivalent at first in the McCain amnesty bill but then it defeated the bill that McCain et al had pushed through the Senate. If this had become law, the people would have had no choice but to throw out both houses of Congress and start over. The people do have lots of power when we "pay attention."

I do have a solution to the problem of 60,000,000 interlopers living in America. We know that with a huge debt on our hands, the American costs are way too high to support the numbers that we must.

We all want the immigration issue solved but not with the illegal foreign nationals owning our homes and forcing us to pay them for living there. My solution in this book tells Washington how to have a pro-American solution to the problem of 60 million illegal residents in our country. Illegal interlopers may not be demanding a deal but if they get no deal at all, the problem of them living 24 X 7 in America will continue. The SR/RV plan is a pro-American deal to offer if the Congress will hear us out!

The immigration issue is being put forth in this book so that we can solve it once and for all for the betterment of US Citizens, not necessarily for resident foreign nationals, though they too get a pretty good deal also.

By demonstrating that our legislators care more about other factors such as reelection and donations than they do about the people, we should be able to mount an effective letter and phone call campaign to get Congress to act on the Resident Visa or the Stipend Return or be ready to face angry voters.

Past president Obama, who theoretically could not run again, used his good friend Hillary Clinton as a surrogate to keep his legacy alive for four more years. Donald Trump spoiled Obama's third victory party and our president is still trying to wall-off America from perpetrators ready to overwhelm our country.

We have more than enough illegal immigrants causing citizens to be out of work in the country right now. Otherwise, our real unemployment picture would not look so bad. Is it not hard to understand that a political party that hates the very notion of slavery, bring more "slave labor" into the country; when we know it will make the problem of making ends meet for American families even worse?

Perhaps too many of US, until things got this bad, had been hoping George would do it! Well, George Washington, one of our finest patriots is long gone, and unless you know of a recent George with the time, it is therefore up to US to do it. Washington and Bush are gone.

Those in Congress who bow to special interests and their big donor base in the swamp should be made to take their final bows if they do not address this problem properly and fairly.

Not only has government at all levels been working against US citizens, the final act of our past president showed complete disdain for real Americans. Without a scintilla of Constitutional authority, in the waning moments of his presidency, yesterday's president ordered well over 30,000 imprisoned criminals in illegal immigration status to simply be released so "they could be reunited with their families in the US."

Among them were rapists and murderers. The homicide and rape victims of our times, got no say. The criminals were released from prison into the US—not deported.

They got to go back on the streets of the US. Some Americans, thinking this was not a good deal for John Q. Public asked: "Did we really need 30,000 more criminals on our streets?"

Our immediate past president thought we should cajole and love the more than 60,000,000 souls in our illegal population, and he acted as if our laws did not apply to him or to the foreign nationals for which he advocated.

Meanwhile more than 30,000 American citizens in prison were not released concurrently with the 30,000 illegal residents so they could be with their families simply because they were not illegal aliens. I agree that American criminals should not be released but neither should foreign national criminals.

There must be a better solution with which all Americans will agree. How about the Stipend Return / Resident Visa Program? Maybe it is worth a chance?

Chapter 6 Some Great Immigration Perpsectives

Mike Blake / Reuters

Mike Blake from Reuters has offered his perspective on the matter. He put forth an excellent article by Victory David Hanson with some of his own comments. Hanson's piece first appeared on the Hoover Institution site. Blake begins by recounting the issue noting that the arguments for ignoring illegal immigration are as well-known as the self-interested motives (Democrats, Republicans, CofC, Business wages, Votes etc.) that drive it.

Open-borders advocates argue that in a globalized culture, which for the record has never existed in any of the neighborhoods in which I lived in Pennsylvania, borders are becoming reactionary and artificial constructs. They should not interrupt more natural ebbs and flows of migrant populations. In other words, come on down. The have nots are being invited to take over the lives of the haves. That's fair?

Suddenly, American workers, who demand a living wage are no longer sought after for many jobs because others will take them and not charge much for their services. And, so a ton of vested interests see a big advantage in dismantling the border. This would mean that employers in hospitality, construction, food processing and agriculture can freely prefer hard-working low-wage immigrants, whose social needs are often subsidized by the government and who are reluctant to organize for higher wages. It is a great deal for business in a world in which only the bucks count.

As always, Democrats step up to the plate as the heroes of the little guy, ready to hit another home run for the people? Which people? The Democratic Party historically welcomes in impoverished immigrants from Latin America and Mexico. It hopes to provide generous social welfare assistance paid for by Americans from all Parties.

What actually happens is not as good as the advertising, however, as the Democrats shepherd the new arrivals and their offspring into what can be seen as "the salad bowl of victimization and identity politics—and thereby change the electoral map of key states from red to blue." If you think this is all about love, and altruism, think again.

La Raza activists who would be pleased to have Mexico annex the US as a nice big fat juicy new territory, see unchecked illegal immigration as useful in maintaining a large pool of unassimilated and poor foreign nationals who look to their group's leaders. This would have the intended result of ensuring the continuance of what has become an industry of ethnic activism and careerism.

Fifty-two percent of all illegal immigrants are from Mexico. This country, due south of the US for its own reasons thinks that it is a good idea to lose its population to the US. And, so it now offers advice to illegal immigrants on how best to avoid U.S. federal immigration authorities. Our neighbor on the Southern border thus has the most to gain by porous borders. It envisions the United States as a relief valve destination to export its own poor and desperate rather than to have them agitate and demand costly social services from Mexico City. How would the latter be good for Mexico?

Victor Davis Hanson is a prolific writer who espouses positions that benefit Americans, not fat cats or political organizations. He asks

"Why should we believe the anti-Trump press?

Mexico pockets about $25 Billion in annual remittances, more or less, "predicated on the unspoken assumption that its poor and hard-working expatriates can only afford to send such vast sums out of the United States through the magnanimity of the American social welfare system that helps subsidize families to free up hard-earned cash." Mexico has learned that its own expatriates are loyal proponents who romanticize Mexico—the farther away and longer they are absent from it. They long for the home country as long as they do not have to go back and sweat it out for a living.

For some reason, even many Americans forget about their brother and sister Americans and they join forces with the radical left-wing ideologues, who want to help those who broke into America to get a share of their neighbor's wealth. Hanson describes this as "the pernicious effects of illegal immigration on the idea of citizenship in a consensual society."

He cites the fact that when countries were formed in the Western constitutional tradition, citizenship was based upon shared assumptions that were often codified in foundational constitutional documents such as our great founding documents. In other words, the people wrote down their laws so that future do-gooders could not do as they please.

Davis Hanson continues this thought in a style of prose that any normal being would be challenged to match:

"**The first pillar of citizenship** is the idea that the nation-state has the sole right to create and control its own borders. The duty of all Western constitutions, dating back to those of the Greek city-states, was to protect their own citizens within clearly defined and defensible borders. Without a finite space, no consensual society can make rules and laws for its own, enhance and preserve commonalities of language and culture, or raise a military to protect its own self-interest.

"Borders are not normally artificial or post-colonial constructs, but natural boundaries that usually arise to reflect common bonds of language, culture, habit and tradition. These ties are sometimes fragile and limited, and cannot operate on universal terms; indeed, they become attenuated when borders disappear and residents not only have little in common, but lack the mechanisms or even the desire to assimilate and integrate their migrant populations.

"When borders are fluid and unenforced, it inevitably follows that assimilation and integration also become lax, as society loses a sense of who, or even where, their residents are. And the idea that the Bill of Rights should apply to those beyond U.S. borders may be a noble sentiment, but the practical effect of such utopianism is to open a Pandora's box of impossible enforcement, affronts to foreign governments, endless litigation and a diversion of resources away from protecting the rights of citizens at home.

"Residency is also confused with citizenship, but they are no more the same than are guests at a dinner party and the party's hosts, who own the home.

"A country reverts to tribalism unless immigrants enter it legally—often based on the host's determination of how easily and rapidly they can become citizens, and the degree to which they can benefit their adopted country—and embrace its customs, language and habits."

This article from which I based this chapter has more from Victor Davis Hanson. He is a great writer and a great thinker. I am presenting much of it below because Davis Hanson and I are on the same side and his analysis is to help us all understand the issue better. My own contribution to my book is that I have a solution for 60 million illegal residents and those to come if we as Americans think we can handle it.

"Related: Victor Davis Hanson: Are we witnessing the end of identity politics?

"The Balkans, Rwanda and Iraq remind us that states without common citizen ties, affinities, rights and responsibilities become fragmented and violent, as their diverse populations share no investment in the welfare of the commonwealth. What plagues contemporary Iraq and Syria is the lack of clearly defined borders, and often shifting and migrating populations that have no stake in the country of their residence, resulting in competing tribes that vie for political control to aid their own and punish the other.

Hanson: "A second pillar of citizenship is the sanctity of the law.

"What also separates Western and Westernized nations from often impoverished and unsecure states is a notion that citizens entrust their elected representatives with the crafting of laws and then show their fealty by obeying the resulting legislation.

"The sanctity of the entire legal system in a republic rests on two important corollaries: citizens cannot pick and choose which laws they obey—either on the grounds that some are deemed bothersome and not in their own self-interest, or on the pretext that they are minor and their violation does not impair society at large.

"Citizenship instead demands that unpopular or unworkable laws be amended or repealed by the proper legislative and judicial branches of government, not by popular neglect or violation.

"Once immigration law goes unenforced, there are pernicious ramifications. First, citizens question why all laws are not equally subject to nullification. If the immigrant is excused from obeying immigration law, is the citizen likewise exempt from IRS statutes or simple traffic laws?

"Second, the immigrant himself adopts a mindset that obeying the law is unimportant. Currently among illegal aliens, there is an epidemic of identity theft, forged government affidavits, and the use of fake social security numbers.

"Open-borders advocates do not disagree that these violations undermine a society, but nonetheless argue that such desperate measures are needed for impoverished illegal aliens to survive in the shadows. Perhaps, but equally true is that once an illegal resident discovers that some of the laws of the host are not enforced, he then assumes others will not be either.

"In truth, illegal aliens lose respect for their hosts, concluding that if Americans do not care to enforce their own laws, foreign nationals need not abide by them either. In reductionist terms, when an immigrant's first act when entering the United States involves breaking the law, then all subsequent violations become only that much easier.

"Besides secure borders and respect for the laws, a third tenet of citizenship is the idea of equal applicability of the law. Citizens in modern Western societies are assured that their laws are applied in the same manner to all citizens regardless of differences in class, gender, race, or religion.

"Illegal immigration insidiously erodes such equality under the law. When millions of foreign nationals reside illegally in the United States, a myriad of laws must be enforced unequally to perpetuate the initial transgression. Illegal immigration does not just imply illegal entry, but also continued illegal residence and all that entails on a daily basis.

"Sanctuary cities protect illegal aliens from federal immigration agencies in a way that is not true of American citizens who arrive at airports and must go through customs, with no exemption from federal agents examining their passports and personal histories. If crimes or infractions are found, there is no safe space at an airport exempt from federal enforcement.

"In California, thousands of illegal aliens have operated automobiles without mandatory insurance, driver's licenses and registrations and, in some municipalities, are not arrested for such violations—even as American citizens who cannot claim such apparent mitigating circumstances are.

"In my own vicinity in rural California, there are hundreds of dwellings where multiple families in trailers, sheds, and garages reside, employing illegal water, power and sewage hookups. Most are more or less left alone by county authorities. The apparent rationale is that such violations are too chronic and widespread to be addressed, or that it simply does not pay for cash-strapped agencies to enforce the law in the case of those who are unable or unwilling to pay substantial fines.

"Either way, the nearby citizen who is hounded by county or federal authorities on matters concerning the proper height of his mailbox, or the exact distance between a new leach line and his existing well, feels that the laws are unequally applied and loses confidence in the value of his own citizenship. He often sees it either as no real advantage over mere residency, or perhaps even a disadvantage.

"In sum, there are several reasons to put a stop to illegal immigration. But among the most important and forgotten is the insidious destruction of what it means to be a citizen.

Victor Davis Hanson is a Martin and Illie Anderson senior fellow at the Hoover Institution.

Thank you, Mr. Davis Hanson, for you most valuable insights.

My buddy Andy G just today, sent me a wonderful email from a legalized American Citizen who knows what it is like to grow up in unfriendly territory and be rescued by American soldiers.

VIETNAMESE IMMIGRANT -- On the difference between legal and illegal.

This is something everyone in America should read.

The town of Prescott Valley, AZ, hosted a Freedom Rally. Quang Nguyen was asked to speak on his experience of coming to America and what it means. He spoke the following in dedication to all Vietnam Veterans. Thought you might enjoy hearing what he had to say:

Start Quote:

"35 years ago, if you were to tell me that I am going to stand up here speaking to a couple thousand people, in English, I'd laugh at you. Man, every morning I wake up thanking God for putting me and my family in the greatest country on earth. I just want you all to know that the American dream does exist and I am living the American dream. I was asked to speak to you about my experience as a first-generation Vietnamese-American, but I'd rather speak to you as an American.

If you hadn't noticed, I am not white and I feel pretty comfortable with my people. I am a proud U.S. citizen and here is my proof. It took me 8 years to get citizenship, waiting in endless lines, but I got it, and I am very proud of it.

I still remember the images of the Tet offensive in 1968, I was six years old. Now you might want to question how a 6-year-old boy could remember anything. Trust me, those images can never be erased. I can't even imagine what it was like for young American soldiers, 10,000 miles away from home, fighting on my behalf

35 years ago, I left South Vietnam for political asylum. The war had ended. At the age of 13, I left with the understanding that I may or may not ever get to see my siblings or parents again. I was one of the first lucky 100,000 Vietnamese allowed to come to the U.S. Somehow, my family and I were reunited 5 months later, amazingly, in California. It was a miracle from God.

If you haven't heard lately that this is the greatest country on earth, I am telling you that right now. It was the freedom and the opportunities presented to me that put me here with all of you tonight. I also remember the barriers that I had to overcome every step of the way. My high school counselor told me that I cannot make it to college due to my poor communication skills. I proved him wrong. I finished college. You see, all you have to do is to give this little boy an opportunity and encourage him to take it and run with it. Well, I took the opportunity and here I am.

This person standing tonight in front of you could not exist under a socialist/communist environment. By the way, if you think socialism is the way to go, I am sure many people here will chip in to get you a one-way ticket out of here. And if you didn't know, the only difference between socialism and communism is an AK-47 aimed at your head. That was my experience.

In 1982, I stood with a thousand new immigrants, reciting the Pledge of Allegiance and listening to the National Anthem for the first time as an American. To this day, I can't remember anything sweeter and more patriotic than that moment in my life.

Fast forwarding, somehow, I finished high school, finished college, and like any other goofball 21-year-old kid, I was having a great time with my life. I had a nice job and a nice apartment in Southern California. In some way and somehow, I had forgotten how I got here and why I was here.

One day I was at a gas station, I saw a veteran pumping gas on the other side of the island. I don't know what made me do it, but I walked over and asked if he had served in Vietnam. He smiled and said yes. I shook and held his hand. That grown man began to well up. I walked away as fast as I could and at that very moment, I was emotionally rocked. This was a profound moment in my life. I knew something had to change in my life. It was time for me to learn how to be a good citizen. It was time for me to give back.

You see, America is not just a place on the map, it isn't just a physical location. It is an ideal, a concept. And if you are an American, you must understand the concept, you must accept this concept, and most importantly, you have to fight and defend this concept. This is about Freedom and not free stuff. And that is why I am standing up here.

Brothers and sisters, to be a real American, the very least you must do is to learn English and understand it well. In my humble opinion, you cannot be a faithful patriotic citizen if you can't speak the language of the country you live in. Take this document of 46 pages - last I looked on the Internet, there was not a Vietnamese translation of the U.S. Constitution. It took me a long time to get to the point of being able to converse and until this day, I still struggle to come up with the right words. It's not easy, but if it's too easy, it's not worth doing.

Before I knew this 46-page document, I learned of the 500,000 Americans who fought for this little boy. I learned of the 58,000 names inscribed on the black wall at the Vietnam Memorial. You are my heroes. You are my founders.

At this time, I would like to ask all the Vietnam veterans to please stand. I thank you for my life. I thank you for your sacrifices, and I thank you for giving me the freedom and liberty I have today. I now ask all veterans, firefighters, and police officers, to please stand. On behalf of all first-generation immigrants, I thank you for your services and may God bless you all.

Quang Nguyen
Creative Director/Founder
Caddis Advertising, LLC
"God Bless America"
"One Flag, One Language, One Nation Under God"

Chapter 7 The Immigration Fix Is In!

The fix satisfies Americans first

The US immigration fix is in and it is very comprehensive, comprehensible, and All-American. As you know by now, it is known as the *Stipend Return / Resident Visa Program* and it is comprised of completely different parts—*The Stipend-Assisted Return Program* and *The Resident Visa Program.*

If you are one of the Americans who is sick and tired of having your lunch eaten and your job taken by a foreign interloper, using your tax money, then you are going to like this fix. The fix addresses each of your pet peeves about foreign interlopers as it outlines a multi-faceted solution that benefits America and American citizens.

It is not pie in the sky. It is designed to work. It will work because while making American citizens #1 again after years of a poor governmental response to our needs, this solution, will also be very popular with the fair-minded members of the underground illegal alien community. It is win-win.

If you are an illegal foreign national, this is your opportunity to be out of the shadows living like all other humans in America. You are going to like this fix. If you are an anchor citizen, or the mom or dad of an anchor citizen, you are going to like this fix. If you are on a temporary or permanent visa and your plan is to stay in this country with a green card, or illegally if you cannot get one, you are going to like this fix. The bottom line is that this fix is in and it is designed to help all constituencies, especially Americans. Isn't it about time? You'll wonder why it took so long

Of course, no fix would be needed if there were no problem. All Americans well aware that there are way too many problems with our immigration system, most of which are because the laws that are in place today have been ignored by Congress and the former POTUS. Obama. Some may be skeptical and ask what good is another law? That is a great question. With the SR/RV Immigration Fix, the law is so specific it cannot be ignored.

However, Congress has yet to agree to any fix and one can easily conclude that the Congress does not want a fix. If Congress will not propose the fix then Houston, we must acknowledge our problem. We must replace our d-nothing Congress. There is no other alternative.

It is good that Donald Trump is now our President, Amen! And thank God. That means the problem has become solvable for all Americans on behalf of America when Congress decides to create and pass the Stipend Return / Resident Visa Program Bill. If Congress fails to act, perhaps it is time for President Trump to find the magic pen and the magic phone as used by Obama.

The Congress knows that in this last election, the people have spoken. Republican legislators should no longer sit idly by and choose not to offer a solution to the people. This new program will solve this huge problem. I do not even want to think about another no action Congress. Clearly, now that we have a President of our choice, the representatives of those parties offering no real solutions are 100% guaranteed to lose their reelection bids.

The people have been mobilized and will have no problem voting them out. Once the people are able to bring the corrupt representatives back home, the government will be able to change for the better. With Donald Trump as President, I expect that the lobbyist-corrupted Congress will work towards solving problems for the people rather than getting thrown out.

The Congress and President Trump must enact this prescribed fix into law. President Trump then must enforce it. This important matter must be solved before America has a higher illegal population than legal.

When states with a majority of illegal foreign nationals begin to petition the US government for the right to secede from the union, we will then see how far this problem will have taken us. Let's not let that happen. We never have to go there. We will prevail. We have the fix. The fix is in. Let's make the fix the law.

Have you ever asked yourself what problems are we trying to solve with the Stipend Return / Resident Visa Program? What are the basic objectives we hope to achieve? Let's look there first.

Look no further than existing documentation from US immigration law or from US agencies. The immigration objectives for America are right here in the immigration oath. It is thing of beauty:

The Immigration Oath

"I hereby declare, on oath, that I absolutely and entirely renounce and abjure all allegiance and fidelity to any foreign prince, potentate, state, or sovereignty, of whom or which I have heretofore been a subject or citizen; that I will support and defend the Constitution and laws of the United States of America against all enemies, foreign and domestic; that I will bear true faith and allegiance to the same; that I will bear arms on behalf of the United States when required by the law; that I will perform noncombatant service in the Armed Forces of the United States when required by the law; that I will perform work of national importance under civilian direction when required by the law; and that I take this obligation freely, without any mental reservation or purpose of evasion; so help me God."

The principles embodied in the "*Oath*" are codified in Section 337 of the Immigration and Nationality Act (INA), which provides that all applicants shall take an oath that incorporates the substance of the following:

1. America first, last, and always
2. Support the Constitution;
3. Renounce and abjure absolutely and entirely all allegiance and fidelity to any foreign prince, potentate, state, or sovereignty of whom or which the applicant was before a subject or citizen;
4. Support and defend the Constitution and laws of the United States against all enemies, foreign and domestic;
5. Bear true faith and allegiance to the same; and
6. Bear arms on behalf of the United States when required by the law; or

7. Perform noncombatant service in the Armed Forces of the United States when required by the law; or
8. Perform work of national importance under civilian direction when required by the law.

The Stipend-Assisted Return Program and The Resident Visa Program fit these important criteria.

USCIS Mission

The most important part of the mission statement of the U.S. Citizenship and Immigration Services (USCIS), the government agency that oversees lawful immigration to the United States is listed under the category of *Vigilance*.

"In this era of increased global threats and national security challenges, we will remain mindful of our obligation to provide immigration service in a manner that strengthens and fortifies the nation. We will exercise a holistic approach to Vigilance as we perform our mission. We will carefully administer every aspect of our immigration mission so that new immigrants and citizens can hold in high regard the privileges *and advantages of lawful presence in the United States."*

From this objective, we can see the major defined purpose of this important Immigration Agency:

- Strengthen the nation
- Fortify / protect the nation
- Maintain a lawful presence
- Be careful who we let into the country (global threats)
- Privilege of citizenship is for citizens

To look at the role even more objectively, it helps to point out that the USCIS mission does not include any of the following notions:

- Family reunification
- Providing gifts of any kind to illegal foreign nationals
- Admitting terrorists into the US
- Changing the demographics of the US
- Permitting illegal aliens to reside and work in America
- Assuring welfare/healthcare is granted to illegal aliens
- Providing any advantages to illegal aliens over citizens

Is illegal immigration a crime?

US law says it is a crime? Does US law matter? It surely did not matter to former President Obama in his eight years as chief executive.

The fact is I should not have had to develop a solution for illegal immigration with as many as 60,000,000 interlopers living in the US when immigration law says this should never have been permitted to happen. FAIR.US is a group on the side of American Citizens on this issue. The following is from their web site. It is their perception about illegal immigration as a crime. It was written in 2013 and continues to apply today. Here it is:

Illegal Immigration is a Crime (2013)

by FAIR.US

> Each year the Border Patrol apprehends hundreds of thousands of aliens who flagrantly violate our nation's laws by unlawfully crossing U.S. borders. Such illegal entry is a misdemeanor, and, if repeated after being deported, becomes punishable as a felony.
>
> The illegal alien population is composed of those who illegally enter the country (referred to as "entry without inspection — EWI") in violation of the immigration law, and others enter legally and then stay illegally (referred to as over stayers). The immigration authorities currently estimate that two-thirds to

three-fifths of all illegal immigrants are EWIs and the remainder are over stayers.

Both types of illegal immigrants are deportable under Immigration and Nationality Act Section 237 (a)(1)(B) which says: "Any alien who is present in the United States in violation of this Act or any other law of the United States is deportable." There are no "buts" in the law.

Illegal immigration is not a victimless crime

Apologists for illegal immigration try to paint it as a victimless crime, but the fact is that illegal immigration causes substantial harm to American citizens and legal immigrants, particularly those in the most vulnerable sectors of our population — the poor, minorities, and children.

Illegal immigration causes an enormous drain on public funds. The seminal study of the costs of immigration by the National Academy of Sciences found that the taxes paid by immigrants do not begin to cover the cost of services received by them. The quality of education, health care and other services for Americans are undermined by the needs of endless numbers of poor, unskilled illegal entrants.

Additionally, job competition by waves of illegal immigrants desperate for any job unfairly depresses the wages and working conditions offered to American workers, hitting hardest at minority workers and those without high school degrees.

Illegal Immigration and Population Growth

Illegal immigration also contributes to the dramatic population growth overwhelming communities across America — crowding school classrooms, consuming already limited affordable housing, and increasing the strain on precious natural resources like water, energy, and forestland. Until the recent economic recession and high unemployment, the immigration authorities estimated that the population of illegal aliens was increasing by an estimated half million people annually.

Illegal Immigration Undermines National Security

While most illegal immigrants may come only to seek work and a better economic opportunity, their presence outside the law furnishes an opportunity for terrorists to blend into the same shadows while they target the American public for their terrorist crimes. Some people advocate giving illegal aliens legal status to bring them out of the shadows, but, if we accommodate illegal immigration by offering legal status, this will be seen abroad as a message that we condone illegal immigration, and we will forever be faced with the problem.

Border Patrol: Necessary But Not Sufficient

The Border Patrol plays a crucial role in combating illegal immigration, but illegal immigration cannot be controlled solely at the border. The over stayers as well as the EWIs who get past the Border Patrol must be identified and removed by the interior immigration inspectors of Immigration and Customs Enforcement (ICE). Today, the policies of the Obama administration are working at cross purposes to this objective. ICE is constrained from detaining and deporting most illegal aliens they encounter with the exception of those with criminal convictions or threats to the national security.

What Can Be Done?

There must be a comprehensive effort to end illegal immigration. That requires ensuring that illegal aliens will not be able to obtain employment, public assistance benefits, public education, public housing, or any other taxpayer-funded benefit without detection.

The three major components of immigration control — deterrence, apprehension and removal — need to be strengthened by Congress and the Executive Branch if effective control is ever to be reestablished. Controlling illegal immigration requires a balanced approach with a full range of enforcement improvements that go far beyond the border. These include many procedural reforms, beefed up investigation capacity, asylum reform, documents improvements, major improvements in detention and deportation procedures, limitations on judicial review, improved intelligence capacity, greatly improved state/federal cooperation, and added resources.

What about The Costs?

Effective control and management of the laws against illegal immigration require adequate resources. But those costs will be more than offset by savings to states, counties, communities, and school districts across the nation.

---End of F-A-I-R description of illegal immigration as a crime-

The US fix, Stipend Return / Resident Visa Program, as we discuss in the chapters of this book is a major cost-saving plan to solve the problem of illegal residency in the US for good. It includes all aspects of the immigration issue, addresses all concerns, and provides a framework that can be used to incorporate new ideas and new programs as they are deemed necessary.

Chapter 8 Objectives of Immigration Law

What are the Objectives? –Otis L. Graham, CIS

The notion of wanting an objective for the big immigration fix that must become law and thus become a major aspect of US immigration policy leads us immediately to a conundrum. In these United States, I am not the person who should be deriving, qualifying or quantifying our current objectives for a sound policy for solving our 60,000,000-resident problem. Before President Donald J. Trump took office, nobody was trying to do any of this?

The set of objectives for immigration policy was partly derived from this analysis by Otis L Graham in 1991. There are some smart and dedicated people in our country who really love America as a great place for Americans. Otis L. Graham is one of these.

In May 1991, Otis L. Graham, of the renowned Center for Immigration Studies (CIS) looked at the immigration world as it existed at that time, and tried to tackle the formulation of an objective—a posteriori from the operational results of the past.

Graham wrote an outstanding analysis of how our immigration objectives have been formed or *not formed* by the agencies that administer immigration law. His article is titled *Rethinking Purposes of Immigration Policy*. It is a perfect title for this groundbreaking work.

Graham's piece is far too big to include in its entirety in this book, but we will show salient parts of his analysis.

In the absence of explicit goals, these results can be seen as the operative or "revealed goals" of the immigration policy. Predominant among these revealed goals is that of ***family reunification*** preferential admission of immediate and extended family members of citizens and legal residents. This was formalized in 1995 after this article was written when the Congress passed The Immigration Act of 1965. This eliminated the national origin quota system that had favored immigrants from Europe to the exclusion of those from other parts of the world.

That system was replaced by a "family preference" quota framework that systematized the sponsorship of relatives by legal immigrants. According to the League of Women voters, "Clearly, the current family reunification system is not working well for many legal permanent residents and their immediate family members." Despite its having messed up our demographics, it still isn't good enough for those that wanted the working system changed in 1995.

The Utopian idea of family reunification as a goal has been an axiom of Congress for nearly four decades of immigration legislation (including the Immigration Law of 1990 and the 1995 revision). It made kinship the determinant of the bulk of our immigrant selection. While you are reading, ask yourself if that is really good for Americans and America.

Additionally, the notion of kinship for whatever reason does not apply to European relatives. It stands to reason that if America was predominantly populated by Europeans why the notion of kinship in family reunification did not apply to Europeans. There had to be tons of cousins, aunts and uncles from Europe waiting to come to America. Why were they left behind? How is it that Mexicans, Latinos, and Asians were the ones who got reunified—to whom?. Just saying? Did somebody make a determination that America was becoming too white? The current mix based on reunification simply does not add up.

There is no God-given right for anybody to be permitted into America. And, so the notion that one person from a family can automatically reunify with the many left behind is absurd. If reunification is the goal, then logic dictates that the one person in America should go back to the home country rather than bring one hundred relatives to our shores. Why bring everybody here? The USA cannot solve all problems by putting its citizens at a disadvantage.

If Americans were aware in the 1990's that the demographics of America from mostly European would change dramatically because of Congress's action, would we have stood for the erosion of the melting pot society and the substitution of the idea that diversity and division should replace unity of purpose? I don't think so.

Even a country as generous as America can give up the advantages of controlling its own destiny when unscrupulous reunifications for example have found as many as 100 family members (some of questionable blood linkage), literally pulled into America by just one relative. When we talk about immigrant selection, of course we are talking about selection for citizenship, and all of the associated benefits thereof. The benefits are to mutually accrue but what benefits the US as a country, has been forgotten along the way.

Ranking second as a revealed objective per Graham's analysis is the admission of refugees. He notes that underlying our generous refugee policy is an array of psychic motives: "affirmations" of American-ness, expressions of national generosity, acclamations of freedom, and votes of confidence in growth and change. Liberals like to feel good about doing good things even if they hurt the bulk of the citizens.

These emotional underpinnings are expressed internationally as the need to vindicate particular foreign policies, to "embarrass" an adversary, or to celebrate America's status as the winning model of what a society should be." Until the notion of terrorism snuck into the equation, America was as good as it gets in terms of refugee acceptance even though in many cases citizen groups felt that too much was unhealthy.

The Germans like to say: "Zuviel ist ungesund!" They also say "Zuviel ist zuviel." We intrinsically know that too much is unhealthy and too much is too much, yet, our leaders continue to punish us with their grand notions of munificence and beneficence, while hiding safe within their gated communities.

In 2017, it no longer can be seen as a badge of honor for a country to admit refugees in large numbers without careful vetting. In fact, it is nothing less than a nation permitting itself to commit suicide. The fact is that in this terrorist-filled world, refugees from regions sponsoring terror may not be who we think they are and they may not be who they say they are. What compelling reason is there for taking that chance and having a terrorist who hates Americans living next door?

President Donald Trump offers a breath of fresh-air and a touch of realism with regard to this cockeyed notion. The President pulls no punches in taking a totally pro-American stance on the issue. *Making America Great Again* does not mean giving everything in America to foreigners.

Americans must be protected from disease and from terrorism. President Trump is against allowing Syrian refugees for example, into the U.S until they can be cleared and verified. Right now, there are no valid records in Syria. Thus, vetting actually is not possible. Why should America be compelled to take in any group of people who may be in conflict with our norms?

President Trump has warned from his first rise to prominence as a presidential candidate that lax immigration enforcement and a too-kind approach to refugees could be a way for terrorists to easily sneak into the country. How many terrorists does it take to kill 50 people in a nightclub in Florida? Would more terrorists than one be needed to kill in other cities?

President Trump is 100% correct that there is no US administrative process to determine who these people are..."we are the worst when it comes to paperwork...this could be one of the great Trojan horses." We all know the old adage about better to be safe than sorry; yet Obama rules for years had us doing the opposite of what was prudent.

A third revealed goal from Graham's analysis of examining the operations impact of immigration, though distant in importance behind either family reunification or the admission of refugees, is to meet labor force needs. Although the 1990 Immigration Law more than doubles the numbers of skills-based immigrants, they will still constitute less than ten percent of the total.

Graham's conclusions and some explanations follow:

> "Another unstated but important result of immigration policy is our long-standing acquiescence in large-scale illegal immigration, effectively an intent to fill the perceived needs of some employers for cheap and docile labor and to avoid offending neighboring countries or domestic ethnic constituencies."

In other words, when this was written, just five years after Reagan's wholesale 1986 amnesty, in which there was much family reunification abuse, government officials had acquiesced to lightly enforce immigration laws instead of doing the job in a robust, meaningful fashion.

In other words, bureaucrats gave themselves permission to not do their jobs according to the law. If the elite establishment had enforced our laws at the border and in the workplace, we would not be suffering the ills of up to 60 million foreign interlopers taking from our shrinking bounty today.

The conclusion that Graham makes is that US policy objectives were overtly permitting this to happen.

> "Though the stated purposes of immigration policy are few and vague, taken together the revealed purposes are powerfully evident. One purpose since 1965, has been the alteration of our demographic future and the delay of population stability. Immigration, and the much higher fertility rates of immigrants, could produce a doubling of the population, to half a Billion, by the year 2080. The demographic transformation of American society is occurring without the consultation or consent of the American electorate."

Did Americans authorize our government to replace people of European descent with those of other nationalities? Would the pre-1965 system, which took into consideration the balanced ethnicity of the current population in determining the proportions of immigrants not have been a better way? How did this happen?

Was there a liberal agenda item to change the makeup of the US demography that snuck into government policy? Why in anyone's objectives, written or otherwise, would there have been a requirement to bring in tons of people from Micksnokoland, even though there were no citizens in the US who were from Micksnokoland?

How in a fair system of ethnic balancing could white people in the US have become an endangered and let me add—a highly disrespected species? Somebody had an ideological agenda that was not shared with the American people or it would have been cut off before it got started. Now, these same people, now exposed, expect Americans to stand by and do nothing. I don't think so.

When he signed Congress's act into law in October 1965, President Lyndon B. Johnson stated that the act "is not a revolutionary bill. It does not affect the lives of millions.... It will not reshape the structure of our daily lives or add importantly to either our wealth or our power." Americans know now that Lyndon B. Johnson was as wrong on that point as wrong could be.

> "Historically, immigration policy was seen as part of "nation-building" to populate a relatively empty land. Are large numbers of immigrants now needed for a land that is built, or even as many believe overbuilt? For some, "nation building," now implies the creation of a more "diverse" nation, energized by a greater mix of ethnic, racial, and national origins. For them, the U.S. constantly faces enervation and stagnation, saved only by steady enrichment of its population from abroad. The idea is odd in a multi-racial, multi-ethnic society of 250 million people."

In other words, the idea of multiculturalism and diversity is like telling all the tribes to maintain their own national identity rather than joining the melting pot of a unified country. This typically does not result in harmony as we find today. This is not good and it is not building our nation in a way in which it can survive and grow and thrive. It is literally killing us.

> "The anachronistic and unintended purposes and goals of our policies demand a fundamental reassessment and reform. The guiding criteria in that renewal must be that immigration policy above all should do no harm: should not harm the conditions or opportunities of the U.S. labor force, should not confound sound

> national population objectives, should not burden social services, and should not exceed the assimilative capacities of American society."

In other words, letting whoever wants to come with unrestricted access into this country as has happened by hook or crook since 1986, does not mean that the country can assimilate them well—especially if those selected want to maintain their separate identity. We have not even included the fact that the majority of the new illegal immigrants as well as the new legal immigrants cannot sustain their own lives and tap into the social welfare system to the tune of hundreds of Billions of dollars per year. America should be for Americans. Let me repeat. America should be for Americans. After all, we built America; not illegal immigrants.

"If immigration policy is to contribute to the demographic future we want, the government must encourage national debate on demographic goals and then select them. Population stabilization, as stated by the 1972 Rockefeller Commission, remains the most cogent and defensible objective, with immigration ultimately set to match emigration."

The 1972 Rockefeller Commission was clear in its objectives for population growth—zero.

> " In the brief history of this nation, we have always assumed that progress and "the good life" are connected with population growth. In fact, population growth has frequently been regarded as a measure of our progress. If that were ever the case, it is not now. There is hardly any social problem confronting this nation whose solution would be easier if our population were larger. Even now, the dreams of too many Americans are not being realized; others are being fulfilled at too high a cost. Accordingly, this Commission has concluded that our country can no longer afford the uncritical acceptance of the population growth ethic that "more is better." And beyond that, after two years of concentrated effort, we have concluded that no substantial benefits would result from continued growth of the nation's population.

> "Current emphasis on immigration as an entitlement of kinship must be recognized as an historical aberration. Labor force needs should once again become the prime determinant of immigration policy, but balancing with greater rigor the desire of employers for cheap, flexible labor with the protection of conditions of U.S. domestic workers. Immigration policy should supplement the domestic labor market with well-targeted, short-term infusions of specialized labor, but without undermining the high standards or incentives that should inform the domestic labor market."

Graham suggests that jobs for Americans are paramount and bringing in cheap labor will help a few Democrat and Republican elitists, but not help the American population at large.

> "The U.S. can either evolve towards a high-technology economy with a labor force of constantly advancing productivity, wage levels, and skills, or it can drift towards a low technology, low-skill, and low-wage economy, marked by widespread job instability and growing income disparity. Immigration policy will be important to the outcome."

Today those at the lowest ladder of the economic spectrum wait for nobody. They hop on a train or get into an inner tube or figure some way to get to America. Then, they go on welfare. How is that good for America?

Democrats think it is good for their long-term ability to hold the important offices in the country. Republicans in the elite establishment want to legalize all illegals and not permit them to make a minimum wage. Better yet, they want to keep the illegal population illegal and in the shadows. They are prepared to continue the status quo if not enforcing immigration law will keep expensive American employees from finding jobs. Meanwhile conservatives and Nationalists want to take back our country and we see President Donald Trump as the only politician in America with a chance of doing exactly that. He needs our help.

Forming immigration objectives & goals

Now that we all have been through the backup work and we have read excerpts from the terrific Graham article, we can again list the objectives. This list is summarized from having examined the many mission statements shown, from the Graham article, and of course from living in the US all my life. This list of the objectives for immigration law is reasonably complete. It is the list from which we designed *the Stipend Return / Resident Visa Program,* comprised of completely different parts—*The Stipend-Assisted Return Program* and *The Resident Visa Program.*

- Assure America and Americans citizens are always #1
- Minimize the tax burden to zero to support immigration policy
- Enforce Immigration Law or Change it
- Secure our borders to protect Americans
- Assure that illegal aliens are not granted amnesty
- Do not permit illegal aliens to reside or work in America
- Assure that applicants for citizenship follow US laws
- Assure that foreign visitors are vetted through a legitimate process
- Assure than Illegal aliens do not vote in any US election
- Assure that Americans have priority for all new jobs
- Assure no path to citizenship for illegal aliens
- Assure welfare benefits go only to us citizen (no freebies)
    - Includes cash, education, healthcare etc.
- Eliminate Birthright Citizenship (Anchor Babies)
- Subsidize Self-Deportation for illegal aliens
- Encourage through large stipends self-deportation for anchor citizens
- Adopt English as America's language
- Collect Back Taxes
- Employer fines for illegal workers
- Provide accountability so America gets paid back for any services

Food for Thought

Frosty Woolridge, a noted philosopher, has a deep perspective on the problem. This quote is from Frosty. It helps all of us get a sense of the reality of the perpetration being played on US taxpayers by our government:

As shown on CBS with Katie Couric this past week, 300,000 pregnant Mexican women cross the border to birth their babies, known as 'anchor babies', in American hospitals at an average cost of $6,000.00 per birth with no complications. If the child suffers heart defects, Downs Syndrome, Autism or any other problems, the costs jump to $500,000.00 with long term care into the millions of dollars. All footed by the America taxpayer!

Not mentioned in Couric's report, that child enjoys free breakfasts and lunches through 13 years of publicly funded education at an average cost of $7,000.00 per year. Additionally, American taxpayers foot the bill for all medical and housing assistance for the child and mother.

More hidden costs add up with ESL classes to teach the child English. Connecticut alone suffers 120 languages in their schools while Colorado suffers over 40 foreign languages that cripple their classrooms.

The list of expenses paid for by American taxpayer soars with time and numbers of illegal aliens. Additionally, legal immigrants, [who themselves are often on public welfare,] sponsor their relatives in chain migration and family reunification at US taxpayer expense.

These immigrants take American jobs while they burn American taxpayer funds for immigrant welfare. This all happens while the US national debt approaches $10 Trillion [now $20 Trillion]. Immigrants flood into this country while jobs cascade out to China where we owe $1 Trillion in T-bills as of 2008. Additionally, we suffer a $700 Billion annual trade deficit.

Summary

In summary, I developed this plan in 2013 but spent a few years perfecting it. I saw all the plans that were out there and no regular Americans, especially those who had been put out of work by the "illegal wage differential," were interested in turning over America to foreigners.

I examined the Gang of Eight plan, existing law, and other notions about how to solve the nation's problem with too many illegal residents. I found that none of the available solutions addressed all of the issues that having 20 million to 60 million illegal foreign nationals in residence brought to America.

As noted previously, I read the Gang of Eight plan in 2013, and I found that it smelled a lot like it was purposely designed to kill America. Why would Republicans John McCain, Jeff Flake, Marco Rubio, and Lyndsay Graham have sold out America in such a harsh way. Rubio lost his opportunities for the Presidential nomination because the people knew he was ready to sell us down the river. Once he went with the Gof8, he was out of my mind for good.

No jobs in this scenario would be left for Americans; newly unemployed Americans would have to pay for newly minted citizens; voting in national elections was not ruled out; 33 million more foreign nationals would be invited. It would cost over $6 Trillion. It was a terrible deal for the country.

I looked at all of the things that Americans did not like and I looked at what the interlopers liked. I figured out a way to permit well-behaved interlopers to be able to stay in America while giving Americans priorities in all ways.

Both of these plans *the Stipend Return / Resident Visa Program* with *The Stipend-Assisted Return Program* and *The Resident Visa Program,* actually will work and will solve the problem of up to 60,000,000 and it will take a huge financial burden off the backs of Americans.

Chapter 9 Gang of Eight Compared to Resident Visa Plan

Gang of Eight not as citizen friendly as SR/RV

We have already discussed the Stipend Return / Resident Visa Program (SR/RV) in enough detail for understanding its precepts and benefits. In this chapter, we compare this innovative notion with the Senate's Gang of Eight fiasco, which Marco Rubio and company tried to ram down our throats in 2013.

So that you know who the treasonous eight scoundrels were who sold all Americans down the river, here is the list. Note there are four Democrats and four RINOS. Eventually, good Americans have to pare these RINOS and mostly all Democrats from the US Senate. They sure do not think like we do.:

- Sen. Michael Bennet, D-CO
- Sen. Richard J. Durbin, D-IL
- Sen. Jeff Flake, R-AZ
- Sen. Lindsey Graham, R-SC
- Sen. John McCain, R-AZ
- Sen. Bob Menendez, D-NJ
- Sen. Marco Rubio, R-FL
- Sen. Chuck Schumer, D-NY

Remember those names. All eight of them are scoundrels. You may recall that in 2013, many of us learned about the Gang of Eight Senators' plan for immigration amnesty for all interlopers. It would have made the Resident Visa Program theoretically unnecessary but it would have gotten us into a deeper mess than we already were in.

Those Americans who think—were not pleased. Low Information Voters accepted it immediately as a good thing. The Marco Rubio

Plan was extremely generous to interlopers and very costly to US taxpayers. It was not a fair deal for citizens of the US. Even Rubio's bank account could not have covered all the added expense.

You are going to love the Stipend Return / Resident Visa Program. This is a 100% comprehensive solution to the problem of having 60 million illegal interlopers living in the shadows of America. That is a lot of shadows. I'd like to take these folks out of the shadows and do something that will both help them and help Americans.

Why would the liberals—Democrats and Republicans in the US Senate do something like this Gang of Eight perpetration? First of all, it is not an accident. It is exactly what they wanted. It still is what they want. It was not forced upon them. Secondly, I am convinced that these rich Senators are so removed from the people at large, they are out of touch and have no idea what is happening in the country.

All Senators should be fired, especially those who do not support our new President Donald J. Trump. When Obama had yet to be replaced, I suggested both houses of Congress should be sent home until further notice. They could not or would not put forth good immigration legislation on behalf of the people, claiming Obama would veto it. Well, Obama is gone. Long live President Donald J. Trump.

We all know that more than any other nation in history, the United States has welcomed immigrants in search of a better life. That is why so many citizens got here over the many years from our founding—and even before—while the colonies were being settled.

For their own reasons, the millions of people who regularly enter the US illegally intentionally choose to violate the core principle of the rule of law in the US, and in fact, they mock and belittle the legal naturalization process. They, as illegal interlopers make demands of our kind and generous host country as if they have an entitlement to free services.

You may recall that on September 18, 2017, DACA protesters shouted down one of their own, Nancy Pelosi who agreed to meet with them. Pelosi was obviously shaken up by the crude interruptions and unruly behavior when ironically, she was on the protesters' side. DACA-supporting protesters stole the show from Pelosi, who tried multiple times unsuccessfully to restore order but instead had to exit when she was outshouted by the crowd.

Pelosi was patient for about 30 minutes during a ceaseless protest. It was no use. She walked out the back door of the building, followed by Reps. Barbara Lee, D-Oakland, and Jared Huffman, D-San Rafael, who were also at the event.

Tucker Carlson of Fox had more compassion for Nancy Pelosi that the DACA recipients and illegal aliens, who were a part of a group of protesters. They were demanding more than Pelosi and the others were willing to give.

Carlson hit the nail on the head in terms of the ingrates in the illegal alien community. They were most disrespectful to a person who has given them just about everything they ever could have asked for. Carlson said DACA protesters showed a "lack of gratitude" for Pelosi and the United States taxpayer, and said that they have no right to demand anything. Carlson made sense. He said that if this situation was occurring in any other country, the citizenry and government would tell the illegal immigrant to "hit the road."

Illegal aliens come to America and want more rights than the citizens of the country. Americans are fed up with it. Pelosi was fed up with it after just thirty minutes. Nonetheless, a continued large-scale influx of new people arrives, without any plan for effective assimilation. In other words, the interlopers want America's benefits but they do not want to adapt in any way to America's culture. Being a good American does not seem to be part of the illegal culture.

I found it difficult to believe that only 40% of green card holders (with permanent resident visas), make the transition to citizenship. They find it comfortable just to stay in the country, collect benefits, and give back nothing. This has occurred over the last 30 years. Today's permanent legal foreign nationals never swear allegiance to America.

As part of the SR/DV recommendations, once the Resident Visa is adopted, there is little need to continue a green card program in which such a high percentage of permanent residents choose not to make the final step to citizenship. Many others would love the opportunity. Once current green cards expire. The permanent resident should get off welfare and apply for a Resident Visa if they merely want to stay in America.

For their own reasons, too many in green card status do not really want to become Americans. They do want to be treated as Americans for benefits and all good things with all due rights, but they are happy holding allegiance to their home countries. The American people are fed up with this, almost as much as we are fed up with illegal interlopers who are on the American dole.

America, once a melting pot!

America long ago became known as the melting pot for people wanting a new place to live and raise a family. In the early days, immigrants left behind their old ways and they became Americans by choice; and they were proud to become Americans. As they say, they melted in. The identity of the pot from which they emerged said: "AMERICAN."

My father was born 102 years ago in 1915 in America, from a pair of Irish immigrants. He loved America and taught me to love this country. As an example, he would get upset if and when I wore an Irish Sweatshirt. He felt I was bragging about being Irish. He cautioned me, his middle son, that I was an American, not an Irishman. Today's illegal interlopers and many green card holders choose not to identify with America. Yet, in many cases, we provide for their every need.

Unfortunately, for Americans, many interlopers and foreign nationals carry resentment and disdain for our country once they get here. Their negative feelings are exacerbated by an unkind Marxist-leaning media that would rather be typing up the news in Soviet Russia than in America.

Only today because of their disgusting narrative to discredit President Trump, do they claim they no longer like the Russians. I believe nothing the media says. I am a Democrat by Party but today's Democrats have no idea who they really are. They surely do not represent main stream America. And, I am beginning to believe that Democratic leaders would not recognize the truth if they tripped over it.

All of these negatives threaten social cohesion and America's civic culture and our sense of common identity. We are not a diverse country. We are a country of diverse peoples with a common purpose and union. E Pluribus Unum. An especially annoying aspect of today's distortion of immigration is that when immigrants, in legal or illegal status are assimilated into the welfare state rather than into a society of opportunity.

Meaningful reform v charade of eight.

2016 was another bloodbath, as conservatives and nationalists-those who believe in America-first, fed up with those who have been shown to be RINOS, demanded change by voting their minds, and they got it. Democrat voters always have moved the country further left to Marxism than most Americans in both parties, think is good. In the 2016 general election, even Democrats and most Conservatives and Nationalists decided that enough is enough. President Donald Trump kicked butt as he was the only Republican that the people (Democrats and Republicans) trusted to execute a pro-America strategy rather than go for a Marxist progressive approach.

Gang of Eight Charade

Instead of offering a meaningful reform, such as a real US Immigration Fix, which would have included a Resident Visa, the corrupt Gang of Eight Senators offered and passed a charade in 2013. Their Bill did not address the intricacies of America's immigration challenges. Instead the Senators offered a magic wand approach.

They pretended that they were solving everything in one colossal bill, with the Democratic Party 100% behind their outlandish overture. Democrats were all ready to take undeserved bows. Yet the

Democrats, my party, chose not to do a thing to help regular Americans.

If I convince you that the Bill was bad, please know that it was actually worse than bad. This Bill, S. 744, would have granted immediate amnesty to the estimated 11 million illegal aliens (20 million to 60 million in my estimates) in the country and it "promised" that in the future the border would be made secure. Promises when dealing with big liars, are never fulfilled.

You may remember the Secure Fence Act, another lie that was passed 283–138 on September 14, 2006 in the house and on September 29, 2006 in the US Senate. President Bush signed the Secure Fence Act, requiring 700 additional miles of double chain-link and barbed-wire fences with lights and camera poles. But Republican Sen. Kay Bailey Hutchison, authored an amendment that DHS would not be required "to install fencing." The Democrat-controlled Congress passed it. In eleven years just 30 miles of the fence has been built. Congress lies.

The Gang of Eight Bill also granted broad new powers to the scandal-ridden Obama Administration and its tab to taxpayers was estimated at $6.3 Trillion. Who's got that kind of money? To me, million as a number still is big and Billion is 1000 times bigger. Trillion is 1000 times more than a Billion.

1,000,000,000,000

Americans said "no" as quickly as the Gof8 Bill was passed in the US Senate. Yet, the Senators chose not to listen to the country. Instead they decided to convince us they were right. They fired off paid ads in the form of propaganda in attempts to sell the Bill to the people as something good for Americans, while the House leadership were still debating the legislation.

Americans wholeheartedly rejected it and the House unexpectedly held its ground. In the fall of 2014 the people went ahead and rejected many of the Bill's proponents and sent them packing. Marco Rubio survived to run for President but his betrayal is forever imprinted on the frontal lobes of conservatives and nationalists.

Congress now works for Congress; not the people

The Senate Bill imposed $Trillions of additional exorbitant costs on the people, and it was filled with political trade-offs and misguided policies. It offered a continuation of benefits (freebies) to all immigrants; participation in social security; no priority of jobs for Americans; a path to voting and citizenship; and a number of other unsavory aspects. It was as if it were written by a foreign power hoping to overthrow the USA from within.

It seemed to many that the US government was trying to bribe the unwelcome interlopers into accepting a sweet deal that with enough chicanery would be welcomed by an ignorant majority of Americans. Americans, however, woke up, and rose to the front of the opposition and proved in this instance that we are not dumb!

And, so, this Gang of Eight Bill was rejected and with good cause. Beware however, as Americans, that our Senators are not on our side in this battle. We must call them to task on their actions on immigration. They are not free agents. They are supposed to be representatives of the people of the US, accountable to us and not beholden to foreign entities.

Initiative, Referendum, Recall, & Impeachment

With a Republican Congress that does not support the President, it is clear that the people need some additional tools of democracy in order to assure that legislators do what is expected. Already, Republicans have balked at the border wall, infrastructure, the budget, Obamacare repeal, it sure would be nice if we the people could use Initiative, Referendum, and Recall at the National level to assure that the will of the people was the mission of our representatives. These tools would make it so that If they did not execute the peoples' will, we could create our own legislation, put petitions on ballots, and in fact we could recall their sorry selves back home and out of office.

Few conservatives would not agree that Democratic leadership in the last twenty years at the federal level has morphed into the Marxist

Party. In this Party remake, individual initiative and survival of the fittest no longer matter.

At the municipal level, the people, Democrats and Republicans have not adopted this hard-left Marxist philosophy and simply want our representatives to be trustworthy and do what is right for us.

In fact, unfortunately for the health of America, most people do not pay enough attention to government. However, never before in our history has vigilance to the actions of public servants ever been more necessary. Politicians of today will take your wallet from your front pocket, stare you in the face, and blame the guy next to you.

Then, they will try to talk you into believing that you did not see what you clearly observed. They will put it on the News as news, though it is fake. There is little value for honesty or the truth in today's Democrat Party.

We get the government we deserve

We get the government we deserve. It is not the people; it is our leaders who have betrayed us on issue after issue. But, it is we the people who must hold the leaders accountable. We must pay attention. The founders told us that is our job. We are too trusting.

We should not be asking politicians for special favors for it emboldens them. If we send them home for good, they cannot hurt us again.

The Marxist-leaning Democratic leadership of today would reject JFK if he appeared as a candidate against Hillary Clinton, the "lady" who was heir apparent in the Democrat Party to replace President Obama. I thank God that it is Donald Trump who took over peaceably on January 20.

In the beginning of this chapter, I promised we would look at Stipend Return / Resident Visa Program and see how it compares to the traitorous Gang of Eight Senate-endorsed program. In the below section, and in the accompanying chart, we can see the utter guano that Marco Rubio and the Gang of Eight tried to force feed Americans.

I contrast Chuck Schumer, John McCain, and Rubio's Gang of Eight Bill with the Stipend Return / Resident Visa (SR/RV) Program. It shows that certain Senators have a different agenda than we do. When their time comes to be reelected, I hope their states cast them out.

In our cursory analysis so far, you may not have been sure that the Stipend Return / Resident Visa (SR/RV) Program was a good deal for you. So, this comparison / summation is designed to open your eyes. if you were ambivalent on the sincerity of the Gang of Eight plan before, these facts should convince you that there was a sellout of Americans in play in 2013, spearheaded by the US Senate. A stodgy group of tired old farts, who no longer care about America, turned against the people.

Thankfully, Americans stopped them this time, and we stopped the Democrats and Hillary Clinton in November 2916. They were prepared to give us more unlawful, unchecked migrations and un-vetted refugees—but we the people picked Donald Trump instead.

Fortunately, forever, President Obama, the one-time Energizer Rabbit, who refused to die many times from the first-time Sarah Palin finished him off in the VP debate, will no longer be around to reject the will of the people by breaking the Constitution. Obama's goal had been to provide the interlopers the freebies they wanted without asking for congressional approval.

This lawless behavior brought about the beginning of the ruination of our country. Since November 8, many loyal Americans are counting our new blessings. I think many of us if invited would have attended the past President's farewell party. After all, we were hoping we could make it happen four years sooner.

So that we know where we would be if Mrs. Clinton, and the Gang of Eight, including wimpy Republicans like John McCain, Jeff Flake, Lyndsey Graham, and Marco Rubio, had their way, we now compare the Stipend Return / Resident Visa (SR/RV) Program with the

Guano Plan of the GO8. It is absolutely a necessary step. We cannot forget who sold us out.

The Gang of Eight didn't play it straight

Americans throughout 2013 heard the constant drumbeat about the Gang of Eight's Amnesty program. Before we go on in any more detail about the SR/RV Program, let's compare bullet by bullet, the Gang of Eight plan (G of 8) with the SR/RV Plan. The bullets are self-explanatory. This may be a real eye-opener for some—especially those who thing Rubio and company are on our side.

2013 Gang of Eight v Resident Visa

	G of 8	SR/RV
Border secure	No	Yes
Jobs	Favors Interloper	Favors Americans
Amnesty	Yes	No
Path to citizenship	Yes	No (almost same as today)
Permanent residents	Yes	Never, renewable visa
Voting	Yes	No, Never
Welfare benefits	Yes	No, Never
Freebies	Yes	No, Never
Anchor babies	Yes	No, stipends to depart
Employer fees/fines	No	Yes -if one employee
Reunification	33M in 10yrs	Not for Resident Visa Holders
Coerced-deportation	None	As needed for violations
Self-return to home	No	Pay nice stipend
Must have healthcare	No	Yes
Must be employed	No	Yes
Must speak English in 2 yrs?	No	Yes
Oath of allegiance	No	Yes, after 1 year
Cost/debt accountability	No	Yes
Taxpayer Costs	$ 6Trillion	Zero
Payback plan	No	Yes
Accountability Database	No	Yes
Interloper fine	Yes	Yes
Employer fine	No	Yes (help finance program)
Back taxes	No	Yes (interview)

Chapter 10 Review Stipend Return / Resident Visa Program

How does the SR/RV Plan actually work?

The one undeniable aspect of the SR/RV plan is that it would relieve the US taxpayer of a huge, unsustainable annual cost burden. The raw cost of services at all government levels to support illegal aliens is from $150 Billion to $500 Billion per year. But, the American taxpayer pays more than just their share of the cost. It affects their income also.

The National Academy of Sciences found that, on average, immigration causes the wages of competing American workers to go down by 5.2 percent. Immigration redistributes approximately $500 Billion in wages from American workers to employers of low-wage immigrants. It helps businesses but not regular Americans who simply can no longer afford liberal plans to pay the full freight for illegal interlopers.

When the SR/RV plan is implemented, all of these costs are gone after just one year. Those who return to the home country cost nothing and those who agree to forego benefits in orger to gain the Resident Visa and come out of the shadows will cost nothing. The impact on regular Americans will be a plus $600 Billion.

When President Trump gets his copy of this book, containing the Stipend Return / Resident Visa Program, the implementation of this program is not far off.

As a side note, when I researched typical passport costs, it was about $120.00 and when I researched typical Visa costs, it was about $160.00, Since most visas are not annually renewable as is the Resident Visa, I would expect the cost of an annual renewal of a

Resident Visa would be about $100.00 Since this is not a full proposal for a Congressional Bill, there are no guarantees on what other levies Congress would places on this program.

The Stipend Return / Resident Visa Plan is process driven. Nothing is by chance. The Resident Visa Holder process begins as you would expect. All 60 million illegal interlopers are given six months to get a special passport. By getting their special passport, they have in essence registered as an illegal alien with the United States Government. At this point, they are legal, and there are no more shadows. Their next step is to apply for a Resident Visa.

Once the six-month period for gaining passports is over, all interlopers by US decree will have a changed status and the status quo will have changed. Either the former illegal aliens have gained legal passports or the former illegal aliens continue to be illegal aliens because they chose to take no action regarding their passport and therefore they remain illegally and are #1 targets for deportation from the United States.

The first step in the SR/RV process for an illegal alien is not very complicated. An illegal alien must first get a special resident passport within a year at various government sites, typically post offices, across the country. This process collects necessary information from the applicant and typically results in the granting of the passport, which is delivered in the mail. Nothing in the passport process, however, happens overnight.

Once a former illegal alien gains their special passport, they are enabled to apply for a Return Home Stipend or a Resident Visa.

The Stipend Return Program is fairly straight forward as the candidate simply brings forth their passport and signs up for the particular Stipend for which they are entitled and their departure is scheduled. They get a free ticket to their home country and a fat stipend.

I see three potential types of beneficiaries who may participate in this program which always means the individual at US taxpayer expense will be provided with all of the customary travel fares and dinners / lunches that are appropriate and scheduled by the US Customs Office.

In other words, the departee will pay nothing out of pocket to arrive in his / her home country.

Th program is designed for the 60 million illegal interlopers residing in the country. However, the Stipend Return program can save the US another ton of funds if it is also used to attract green card holders on welfare, and anchor babies on welfare. When they return to their home countries there is no longer a cost for welfare.

The three categories are as follows:

1. Current interlopers
2. Legal green card holders on welfare
3. Anchor babies at any age, including children supervised by a legal or illegal parent.

The recommended stipend for each of the three categories is as follows:

1. Current Interlopers	$20,000
2. Legal Green Card Holders on Welfare	$30,000
3. Anchor Babies or Adults	$50,000

Anybody opting for a stipend in any of the above categories are prohibited without special petition from every returning to the United States for any reason. Any debt accrued that is accounted for in the Accountability system must be collected prior to any request for readmission to be examined.

Other uses for this program to make a point

No new system should be designed with just one objective when there are so many clearly similar objectives known at the time of design. For example, I see five distinct sets of people data and a catch-all that should be part of the same system design. They are as follows:

1. 60 million illegal interlopers who are in country today
2. Illegal visa over stayers
3. Legal visa holders

4. Green card holders and other legal residents
5. Anchor babies even if over 21 yrs. of age
6. Other foreigners in the US

I place other at the bottom of the list as a catch-all. I am sure that there are some off the wall cases of foreigners such as diplomats etc. that do not demand a separate system.

The 60 million interlopers

Before I continue, may I remind you again that my concern in this book is not border security; it is not E-verify; it is not the visa system; and it is not green card holders or other legal residents. My objective is to come up with a system design and I have done that. It solves the problem of the 60 million illegal interlopers in this country today. We are a smart enough country that we should have solved this years ago but we obviously have not had officials with a will to do so. This is another reason I thank the Lord for a man so able and willing to pitch in as President Trump.

With a Stipend Return Program and a Resident Visa system operational, there may be other opportunities for synergy by creating a base system that will solve the problem for all types of permanent resident or temporary resident foreigners or illegal-entry foreigners residing in this country at this time and times in the future.

Suppose With 5 million interlopers signed up and accepted the Stipend Return payment. It would cost $100 Billion to implement in the first year (5M X 20K). This would save the US treasury $50 Billion the first year (5M X 30K – 20K) = $50 B. In subsequent years, it would save another $250 Billion per year.

The stipend would cost the US about $100 Billion to implement but it would all come back by not having to pay annual benefits. It would all be reclaimed in the second year of the program and every year thereafter.

The short view of the program is that after gaining the passport for Stipend Return, the new registrant signs on the dotted line and agrees to abide by the terms of the program, including no lawsuits. The payment occurs when the interloper reaches the home country within 6 months of the agreement and collects the stipend.

Accept the Stipend Return or Apply for the Resident Visa

The SR/RV plan is very generous in its desire for unhappy illegal interlopers to go back to their home countries and reestablish their lives. As such, after registration, the US will provide a special credit card that can be used only by the interloper and only for authorized travel to their home country. The stipend will be available at the interlopers' bank in the home country.

All interlopers with passports for the Resident Visa, who after vetting are approved and not deemed to be bad guys can sign up and pay the fee for the Resident Visa. This enables them to stay in the US under the terms of the visa. This visa may be renewed annually. As noted, after year 1, an oath of allegiance must be taken to get the first renewal, and after year two, the Resident Visa holder must pass a literacy test and an English test in order to be accepted for renewal for the third year.

Special conditions may be included by US officials in the event time expires at any stage of the process, and the registrant has neglected the call and has simply chosen not to move forward to complete the process. Those who do not pass either the English test or the literacy test may opt for a one-time year extension in order to pass the tests. If they choose not to take the extension, they will automatically be enrolled in the Stipend Return program. If they fail to arrive in their home country under the program, they will receive no stipend and will be deported in the customary fashion.

Is the Stipend Return program acceptance automatic?

Yes, it is automatic. There is no reason to deny such interlopers their opportunity to go home at this time. So, if they apply, they will be accepted.

Is the Resident Visa program acceptance automatic?

No, it is not automatic. Besides the casual passport interview, two additional interviews are required. The first is general vetting about worthiness to be part of the program. The second is to determine finances and debts that may be deemed payable to the US under the accountability system. Even the gang of 8 program had a $2,000 fine imposed for the illegal entry. Whatever fees or fines are determined by officials will be assessed for those qualifying for the Resident Visa during the finance interview. The payments can be made over time so as to not be extremely burdensome.

Two Resident Visa interviews (aka double vetting)

Interlopers, who choose to gain a Resident Visa go through a process that includes obtaining a special passport and they undergo several vetting interviews to prove their worthiness in America and to American citizens. During the interviews, the applicants agree to a number of stipulations that permit them to get out of the shadows permanently and begin to enjoy all benefits of holding a Resident Visa as a temporary guest of the Unites States of America. The shadows will be eliminated once the Resident Visa is in force.

The interviews will be extensive though much of the information may be collected online at the applicant's choosing. The precepts of the "deal" are clear. Among all other detailed stipulations, the applicant also agree to pay an annual renewal fee in addition to whatever fines, fees, & taxes are determined by US officials.

In order to be admitted, the applicant agrees to be "well-behaved." The idea of "well-behaved" is a notion that is to be defined each year by the immigration service of the US. The applicant also agrees to hold a job; to obtain his or her own healthcare insurance; and to never vote while being in Resident Visa status.

Additionally, the applicant promises to take no freebies ever from the US, States, or Municipal Governments. In other words, they agree never to take benefits from the US ever again—especially in healthcare, education, and cash payments.

They agree that they will not ever claim federal child credit to gain unwarranted tax refunds as has been frequently done in the past. Only US citizens can receive benefits from any of the US systems, including the IRS. Most importantly they promise to stay clean and be good residents of America.

In case you may think that tax credit fraud is uncommon and would be chump change if we stopped it, think again. In 2011, your friendly IRS sent more than $46 million in tax refunds to 23,994 "unauthorized" alien workers who all listed the same address in Atlanta, Ga. Can you imagine how widespread this type of fraud actually is. This was uncovered in an audit report by the Treasury Inspector General for Tax Administration (TIGTA).

Those applying for a Stipend Return or a Resident Visa, are not obligated to agree to any of the stipulations which are put forth. However, if they decide not to abide by all the stipulations, by way of their applications, by default, they have agreed to self deport with no stipend.

In this full process, there will be fines and fees up front besides the passport and visa fees depending on what government officials feel need to be collected. If such amounts cannot be paid immediately, they may be "charged" to the accountability system. Besides fines, etc. taken on account if the applicant has no resources, the Resident Visa Holder must pay out of pocket an estimated $100.00 renewal fee for each year of approval.

Their financial database record called an Electronic Accountability Record (EAR) and smart card information will be updated with each renewal and major change to demographics. If they abide by the rules and renew their status every year, they can live in the US forever, without fear of deportation. But, they must renew their application in person every year.

Otherwise, they have chosen to ignore our generous hand, and deportation either via the Stipend Return Program or via self-deportation is the only option available. It is a simple plan; a simple process; that is, it. It is fair to all. It solves the problem of as many as 60 million interlopers for good. You have just read about the essence of the program. The Stipend Return / Resident Visa plans are such good ideas that they can help in other areas to assure the US gets all the benefits.

Children

Children, must also register for one of the two new programs. They too must get passports and be approved. Anybody 18 years of age or older is considered an adult.

The SD / RV program solves the problem for DACA children also. As a DACA concession, the Resident Visa will be no charge for the first five years. Those in the DACA program also qualify for the Stipend Return Program if they do not want to stay in the US.

Summary of benefits:

- No more shadows
- No more freebies
- No more cost to Taxpayer

Stipend Return / Resident Visa Plan Summary

In summary, the major points in the SD/RV plan are as follows:

- Addresses all American concerns on America's side
- Resident Visa gives right to reside in America and hold jobs
- No freebies; no voting; no citizenship; jobs for citizens 1st
- All applicants first must obtain special passport
- Can choose to take a stipend and return to home country
- Stipend Return paid in home country
- All applicants for Stipend Return accepted.
- Can choose to obtain a Resident Visa
- Requires 2 vetting interviews; pay fees, fines.
- Interview 1 – demographics; Interview 2 – financial
- All interloper debt kept in Electronic Accountability Record
- Debt collected slowly over time
- Must get special passport in one year
- Must pay any assessed fines, costs, back taxes

Program participants are on temporary visas and not eligible as benefit recipients

Before an applicant signs on the dotted line for their special passport, and Resident Visa, they must agree to a number of provisos. By signing, they accept each and every proviso and future added provisos. They cannot pick and choose. They are not citizens and do not have the rights of citizens. The taxpayers of the US as citizens are the masters. These provisos include the following:

- Learn to speak English in 2 years
- English test each renewal
- Participants have no citizenship rights
- A child resident must get a Resident Visa
- Guests may have children in US but must agree their offspring are not anchor citizens. They are automatic Resident Visa Holders.
- Program is at pleasure of Congress & President
- Must renew status once a year.

- Must permit Photo ID & databases to be updated
- Must pay annual fee & something towards debt.
- This is not an amnesty program.
- Debt is accountable and payable
- Debt does not require immediate deportation
- No US family reunification provisions as Reagan amnesty
- US will assist with family reunification in home country
- Special program for former Anchor Babies
- Visa holders cannot vote
- Visa holders May keep jobs at minimum wage or more
- For new jobs, American Citizens have preference
- Requires strict enforcement of all current laws
- Obama immigration amnesties repealed
- Other stipulations as defined by Congress and President Trump

Chapter 11 Green Card Elimination?

Do we still need the Green Card Visa?

Most immigrants who wish to make their home in the United States know that becoming a Lawful Permanent Resident is the first step. Today, without the new Resident Visa as proposed, this status is key to becoming a legal resident and to ultimately become a citizen. It allows the person to live in the U.S. on a permanent basis (A ten-year status that is renewable)—so long as he or she does not commit any crimes or other violations that would result in deportation.

A person in this status may by choice move on to become a citizen of the US. But, thirty-five to forty percent of green card holders are here for years and never choose to take the steps towards citizenship.

A green-card-holder is another name for a permanent visa holder. The permanent resident is given an identity card that was once green, and the card is still popularly known as a green card.

Qualifying for a green card to live in the United States can be a challenge. The law strictly defines the categories of people eligible for green cards, and in some categories, the law limits the number of green cards that can be given out each year. The application process is also usually lengthy and difficult.

In understanding this matter fully, we must realize that, no matter what category one might fall in to, you can be denied a green card if you are found "inadmissible" to the United States. The grounds of inadmissibility found in the U.S. immigration laws are meant to protect the United States and its citizens from anyone who is a perceived risk due to a criminal or terrorist background, past immigration violations, communicable health problems, inability to support themselves financially, and so on.

Major Change to Green Card System

As an adjunct to the Resident Visa program, I am suggesting that Congress eliminate the green card program and create a version of the Resident Visa that has all of the requirements of the green card but does not give permanent residence. Those who are in the US under a legal permanent resident visa (green card) can get a "green" Resident Visa card, which provides all of the rights of the green card except permanent residence. Since there is no permanent residence, there would be no welfare or cash payments or any benefits.

Less than 2/3 of the green card holders move on to become citizens. And, so, the Resident Visa Program would need to be tweaked just a bit to add the criteria for green cards. Any person who would have gotten a green card in the past would, in the future get a "reen" version of the Resident Visa Card, with a specially designated code that enables them to become citizens. Other Resident Visa Holders would have no opportunity for citizenship.

Right now, there are few requirements the permanent residents need to meet in order to apply for U.S. citizenship. This would not change when the green cards are part of the Resident Visa Program. Applicants with the "green" Resident Visa would need to show that they were present in the U.S. for 30 months within a five-year period before they could apply for citizenship. Likewise, those applying for U.S. citizenship based on their marriage to U S citizens, would have to establish that they were present in the country for 18 months within the three-year period. That's it.

Permanent residents of today can receive benefits so the big change in making them temporary residents under the Resident Visa Plan is that they would no longer get benefits. Since the length of a permanent visa today is 10 years and it is renewable, when the ten years expires for those in the US with an original green card, these green cards will not be renewed. Instead, they will be converted to temporary visas. Of course, they also have the option of bypassing the Resident Visa and opting for the Stipend Return Program.

We can still call it the Green Card if we choose. This would distinguish those who can move on to citizenship from those who were legalized as temporary residents under the SR/RV program.

The below considerations are in effect today from US documentation are not new proposals brought forth for the SR/RV.

The following classes of immigrants are currently eligible for green cards and these criteria would be used for those applying for the "Green" Resident Visa Program.

Immediate Relatives of U.S. Citizens

One of the most widely used categories of green card eligibility is immediate relatives of U.S. citizens. Immediate relatives include:

- spouses and recent widows and widowers of U.S. citizens
- children (unmarried under age 21), stepchildren, and stepparents as long as the marriage occurred before the child was age 18, and
- adopted children if the adoption takes place before age of 16.

There is no limit to the number of immediate relatives who can receive green cards each year.

Preference Relatives of U.S. Citizens and Lawful Permanent Residents

A limited number (480,000) of green cards are given out to other relatives of U.S. citizens and lawful permanent residents, referred to as preference relatives. The result is long waits in most categories. The green cards (otherwise known as immigrant visas) are given out on a first come, first served basis, so the earlier an intending immigrant's relative turns in the initial visa petition (Form I-130), the sooner the immigrant can apply for a green card.

The wait tends to range from three to twenty-four years. Brothers and sisters of U.S. citizens wait the longest.

The following are the preferences in order of preference:

1. Unmarried children of a U.S. citizen who are age 21 or older
2. Spouses and unmarried children of a Green Card Holder (this includes two subcategories, 2A and 2B; children over age 21 are in category 2B, and wait longer than those in 2A)
3. Married children of at least one U.S. citizen parent
4. Sisters and brothers of U.S. citizens, where the citizen is at least age 21

Employees and Workers

A total of 140,000 green cards are available each year for people whose job skills are needed in the U.S. market and who offer skills which an employer cannot find from the local market of U.S. workers. In most cases, a job offer is required before the immigrant can seek a green card, and the employer needs to begin, and actively participate in the application process.

In three categories, however, a job offer is not required. These include investors (fifth preference, described below); workers of "extraordinary ability" (a subcategory of the first preference priority workers' category described below); and workers with "exceptional ability," a subcategory of the second preference category.

Given the limited number of green cards available to workers, it can take many years to receive a green card through this process, depending on which preference category you're in.

The following are the preferences in order of preference:

1. People of extraordinary ability in the arts, science, education, business, or athletics; outstanding professors and researchers; and managers/executives of multinational companies.
2. Professional with advanced degrees or exceptional ability.
3. Professional and skilled or unskilled workers.

4. Religious workers and various miscellaneous categories of workers, as well as so-called "Special Immigrants" (described below).
5. Investors willing to put $1 million into a U.S. business, or $500,000 in business that's in a locally depressed area. The investment in the business must create at least ten new jobs.

Green Card Lottery: Diversity Visa

There are 50,000 green cards available each year through a questionable mechanism called a diversity visa, popularly referred to as the green card lottery. Think about how fair this is to people waiting in line.

Only citizens of certain countries may apply. The countries on the list are those that have, in the past, sent the fewest numbers of immigrants to the United States.

Applications are accepted online for one month, usually toward the end of the year. Applicants must also meet certain educational qualifications. The application process is free. No wonder millions of people apply each year, making the chances of winning quite slim. Also, even if you are one of the lucky few selected, realize that you'll be in a race with other winners to get the process done on time. Many people are left out by the end of each cycle, often because of the slow-moving government bureaucracy.

Special Immigrants

This category contains an odd mix of visa types, many of them too narrow to be useful to more than a few people. Special immigrants include:

- Religious workers (clergy as well as other people in a "religious vocation," such as religious instructors, cantors, and workers in religious hospitals).

- Foreign medical graduates who came to the U.S. before January 10, 1978 on an H or J visa and meet various other conditions.
- Former international U.S. government workers.
- Retired employees of international organizations.
- Persons declared dependent on a juvenile court.
- Service people with 12 years' duty.

Refuge and Political Asylum

The U.S. government offers refuge to people who have a fear of, or have experienced, persecution in their home country based on race, religion, nationality, political opinion, or membership in a particular social group. With concern for terrorism a paramount notion in the minds of Americans. many believe that this notion is today being abused by government officials in favor of foreign nationals and against the citizens of the US

The U.S. government sets a different limit on refugee admissions -- those who come from overseas -- each year. There is no limit on the number of people who can, from within the U.S., apply for asylum each year. Refugees and asylees can apply for a green card one year after receiving their status.

If Resident Visa Replaced Green Card

No more green cards would be issued when the Resident Visa Program Begins. Instead those who would have qualified for a Green Card may sign up for a special form of the Resident Visa. Unlike the original Resident Visa Program introduced in this book, the Special Resident Visa Program will be available only to the following classes of people:

- Immediate Relatives of U.S. Citizens
- Preference Relatives of U.S. Citizens and Lawful Permanent Residents
- Employees and Workers
- Green Card Lottery: Diversity Visa
- Special Immigrants
- Refuge and Political Asylum

Chapter 12 Review of The Resident Visa Approval Process

Once you get your special resident passport

Once somebody is approved in a two-interview vetting process after receiving their passport and they get their Resident Visa, they must pay fees and fines and back taxes determined from the financial acceptance interview. If the new guest cannot pay all that is due, it is recorded in the EAR and the debt accumulates in the ACCT database.

As noted previously, this is an accountability database set up to store demographics and amounts due to the government for fines and back taxes, etc. A US agent schedules a payment plan if necessary, though the desired result is immediate payment during the aspirant interview for the Resident Visa.

In addition to being able to live in the US without harassment, with a Resident Visa, a former interloper can work legally in America. They may keep their jobs and they may compete with Americans for advertised jobs with Americans always being given a clear priority. More than likely, wages will increase as Resident Visa Holders can no longer be paid under the table once they are legal entities in the US. This is another advantage to what will become the former interloper community.

Americans are first in line for new jobs

For Americans, we do not get the jobs now held by interlopers. I would not even agree to that if I were an interloper. Interlopers may keep their current jobs. No interloper would sign up for this program without being able to continue working. It is reasonable to expect that the average wage of Resident Visa Holders will increase.

Americans may choose to keep their current jobs of course and may apply for any new job once held by an interloper who either voluntarily deports, is deported, or who is not approved for a Resident Visa. The difference from the past is that any new job opening goes to a qualified American before any visa holder of any kind.

During the one-year passport period, interlopers can avoid rapid deportation. Those who are not actively trying to become part of the program and who do not have passports may have their number called by ICE and therefore, it behooves them to get their special passports early in the year. Only those with passports will qualify to receive the $20,000 Stipend Return.

Of course, no interloper may apply for the Stipend Return or the Resident Visa without first gaining a passport.

The process will be designed to be low cost in its implementation so that there is not a huge administrative nightmare associated with the program. My career in IBM involved designing first of a kind, innovative, and complex systems so I am confident this can be done with minor modifications to existing systems, a proper plan and great execution.

It will be an efficient bureaucratic process that incorporates online offsite data collection and efficient pre-programmed interviews with federal agents or designated officials at another federal level. Any extra costs associated with this process will be paid for by the interloper.

There is no such thing as a citizenship path for Resident Visa Holders. They do not qualify. In other words, a short transitional path to citizenship is not available. However, a Resident Visa Holder has no less stature than a foreign national in his or her home country and thus may use the same process as exists today for everybody else to go back home to begin a path towards US citizenship. There is no line jumping.

For the home countries, this program provides assurances that somebody in the US who has been in an illegal status cannot jump ahead of those waiting at home. To say differently, all existing home country citizenship candidates are ahead of a new Resident Visa Holder.

Likewise, there is no path to a green card from Resident Visa status. In fact, I have recommended the elimination of the permanent resident visa. Nothing is changed regarding the procedure to become a citizen. The candidate must wait in line as all others for citizenship. Yet, if willing to accept Resident Visa status, the shadows are 100% gone.

There is no voting – ever. This option is simply not available. Only citizens can vote in any US election at any level. This eliminates the possibility of foreign nationals taking over the government of small towns or even large towns.

Why implement the Stipend Return / Resident Visa Program?

From the very first page of this book, we have been explaining the answer to this question. In a nutshell, it is a merciful way to handle interlopers legally without requiring coerced deportation. The process helps Americans and interlopers and does not harm either. Nobody in the US, including the interlopers have gained by having them living in the shadows.

Because this will be a no-benefit program, many interlopers may choose a Stipend Return—typically with a $@0,000 stipend. In most cases, normal transportation costs will be covered by the US government. Some may qualify for additional loans and other stipends.

Without a fix, the existing mess created by past presidents and exacerbated in the Obama years, has the potential to create revolution in this country. The citizens are sick and tired of being pushed around by a government that favors foreigners over Americans.

Even conservatives do not have the stomach for mass deportations. But, the media's constant message of unfairness helps promote this feeling. We have already demonstrated that the cost of deportation is more than offset by the savings to the US taxpayer. In fact, it is a substantial net plus for Americans. With the SR/RV, deportation is mostly voluntary and encouraged under the Stipend Return program. It is not often coerced.

Chapter 13 Accountability for Interlopers

Should not all loans require payback?

When a good friend asks for some money to help her through a crisis, if you are like me, you give her what she needs to the extent you can afford it. After all, you too may be in the same situation in the future. When you do this, do you simply withdraw from your account and add it to theirs? Is that the last time you expect to ever see the amount of the help even if the friend becomes the next Donald Trump? Have you no claim to what you have given? Or, do you and your friend know there is a debt due?

Other than for family matters, which are often unaccountable, most friends help friends as much as possible financially but the amounts given are expressed or implied loans, and both parties know a payback is expected if things get better. There are no huge gifts from one to another. Yes, eventually loans may be forgiven but by the choice of the lender not the borrower.

There is an old saying that is reflected in the song, *Robinson Crusoe*, sung by Al Jolson. When he described his pal, Friday, to show that he was a good man, in the song, Crusoe noted that "*He did not borrow or lend.*" You remember in Shakespeare's Hamlet, 1602, Polonius said: "*Neither a borrower nor a lender be…*" Borrowing and lending are tricky deals among friends. In the big financial institutions, you know as a borrower, you pay every last penny plus interest.

How is it that the government sends huge amounts of dollars and in-kind contributions to citizens for their welfare – cash payments, rent subsidies, medical payments, etc. Would you believe that the government doesn't keep track of any of this? There is no database anywhere yet, the government has given away $Trillions of unaccountable benefits. To whom. How much? When? Why? It is safe to say that nobody knows!

May government actually give gifts?

Are these benefits gifts from the government? Who is the government? Are they gifts from congresspersons? Are they gifts from the President? They are definitely gifts because nobody in the government, after the huge gifts are sent out every week, knows to whom the gifts were sent, or who received the gifts. They never ask for the "gifts" to be paid back. Is this a good system for America?

And, so suppose just a day after a $2,500 gift goes to Joe Dokes, Mr. Dokes also receives a check from the Powerball Lottery for $7,300,000,000. Would you expect Joe Dokes to choose not to cash the government check, or return the automatic deposit? It is not likely, because Dokes always viewed cash and benefits from government as gifts; not loans.

Likewise, the Big Six auditing firms checking the US Treasury accounts receivable would not find any entry indicating that Joe Dokes owes the government $2,500.00. Why? Because it was a gift! Now, if we chose to call these amounts helping loans instead of gifts, with no corresponding change in accounting (still no tracking), I would bet a small percentage, but at least a few people nonetheless, would pay back the government when extremely better times came about?

Why do we treat them as gifts? The recipient certainly did not earn a gift or a benefit as in Social Security, Medicare, or Unemployment Compensation. I do not even want to know the answer. I am sure that it is tough enough being a great politician giving one taxpayer gift after another to one voter after another to ever suggest that the indebted voter might actually ever; be compelled to repay the gift!

Who gets the gifts?

Who knows? There is no list? If the government does not know to whom they give the gifts or the values of the gifts, then collection or a requested repayment is impossible. The givers of the gifts, the politicians, can never be blamed, since nobody will ever be asking and therefore, nobody will be asked for a loan repayment.

Welfare and medical services and 118 other US benefits are simply free for the taking, and they are killing US. You bet they are. Not one dime has ever been accounted for or collected on taxpayers' behalf. Yet, we as a country are $20 Trillion in debt.

Politicians actually believe money grows on trees.

There is no accountability because Congress wants it that way. Congress wants to be duly recognized by the receivers of the largesse as the grand giver. They want people to feel indebted to them, though it is not them, it is you and I, the American taxpayers who fork out the dole received by interlopers and others with no accountability.

They get to buy votes with taxpayer dollars with no repayment required. No government "gift" should be an eternal gift. Government should not be permitted to give "gifts." Find gifts in any articles of the Constitution or the Bill of Rights, or even mention in the Federalist Papers. You won't! It was not how our country was founded.

Illegal foreign nationals and many others, with no hope of ever making a payback, get gifts from the taxpayers via Congress also. Who is being played for a fool here? Such interlopers are instructed by other interlopers to take the money and run, and don't worry…be happy! They know that the US will have no idea who they are.

The Resident Visa Plan solves this problem for good. We track immigrant / interloper / guest debts. That is why this plan will be hard to get introduced or passed in Congress without Americans getting involved. Of course, the plan would work even if the accountability were taken away so let's not forget that. But, it helps to remember that Congress loves giving away your money!

Cost Accountability

Accountability for Resident Visa Holder debt is a major feature of the Resident Visa Plan. However, it would help all of America if it became a part of all US welfare plans eventually. I am not talking about earned things like Social Security, Medicare, and Unemployment Compensation. Anything that helps anybody think that not working is the preferred action to assure benefits is on my target list. It should be on your target list also.

And, so with regard to the Resident Visa Plan, any aspirant who becomes a visa holder can stay in the US until asked to leave for some violation of the requirement to be well-behaved. They are on their own financially just like you and I

When Resident Visa Holders who really try to keep up with their payments to taxpayers—run into issues in repayment, I would recommend that they should not be treated too harshly at first. As soon as they are back on top, they should be required to get back on the payment track as soon as possible.

Their financial transactions leading to debt to the US Treasury, under the plan, would all be captured in their EAR (Electronic Accountability Record) in the ACCT database. This database is the proof that there is no free lunch. There is no amnesty. There is no welfare state just for having been an interloper who became a guest. Those days are gone. Everything is accounted.

Eventually, former interlopers would have to pay this back or figure out the best way to leave the country.

Keeping an accounting of interloper debt is as great a start for this program and for the United States as is granting passports to the 20 to 60 million interlopers for the first time. Once debt is accounted, it can then be collected, even if it is piecemeal.

Attempts to collect need to be made that are not harassing to citizens or newly minted visa holders to assure payment or partial payments on a regular payment plan. Over a proper amount of time, Resident Visa Holders must pay back all accrued debt on their record and any future debt they may be permitted to accrue. Heirs and assigns should be required to pay some portion of an estate to reduce the debt balance of a deceased.

Access to database records

Each record in the SR/RV database as well as the ACCT database will have multiple access keys. An ID #, which is like a social security number is appropriate. Of course, the ID should not be a social security number. The SR/RV # will be encoded magnetically in the ID card in the same fashion as card numbers are recorded in charge cards.

A bar code, an RFID chip, fingerprint, retina, and facial scans will also be recorded from the interviews and they will be verifiable. They will come into play from the point of the registration process and the guest photo ID card. Any of these ID features will be able to be used to access data in the SR/RV or ACCT databases for those with authority to do so.

The data can be fetched therefore via biometrics or a verified guest number. As noted above, but repeated here for effect, I would advise that social security numbers not be used for Annual Guests. If an interloper or guest can be identified by a finger print, they can never snooker the US system into thinking they are a dead guy or somebody else whose ID they may have stolen.

Americans do not want to be messed with!

Reality says that in a US in which most people do not want to deport the poor souls living in the shadows, how do we get the "shadow people" to begin paying US back for what they have taken? Americans are not happy about the authorized theft of taxpayer dollars in the form of gifts that have been granted by the prior POTUSes and the Congress.

What if we came up with a standard way of paying back US taxpayers for those interlopers who eventually become Resident Visa Holders?

What would it look like? What would the standard required payback actually look like? Let's take a shot at building the scenario in simple terms:

The standard payback:

- Must pay 10% of debt or 10% of income each year
- Requirement to renew as a Resident Visa Holder.
- Can gain special repayment waivers for hardships during annual interviews.
- Additional processing cost- waivers added to EAR
- To repeat: No free lunch!

Let's review some of the jobs notions for the SR/RV.

SR/RV favors Americans for jobs!

The following list summarizes the impact of The Resident Visa Plan on Jobs:

- Pre-SR/RV --Favors Interloper; cheap wages
- Post SR/RV -- Favors Americans, not mean spirited
- SR/RV = Jobs much more available for Americans
- SR/RV = Visa holders may keep current jobs
- SR/RV = Citizens prioritized v Visa holders for new jobs

Do Americans feel taken?

Americans are not dummies. We just have been lulled over a number of years of good government that such good government would continue. It has not continued. In fact, today's style of government is unacceptable for honest Americans. Who in the US can be pleased with this system of government given to us today by corrupt, arrogant, and greedy politicians?

In the notion of no freebies, as a requirement of the SR/RV, a corollary, is that every Resident Visa Holder pays for everything. Let's honestly ask ourselves: "If not them, then whom?"

Place yourself in the role of a visa holder, recently freed from the shadow of deportation. If you are a Resident Visa Holder, having once broken into the USA, and now, having broken away from your days as an interloper, should you not be pleased?

If you are not pleased, should you expect that somebody who you have never met will step up and say they will pay all your expenses because you would like to live in America, expense free? Sorry, unless you find such a person, it would be best to appreciative your new freedom. Your expenses are on you, however—nobody else.

Government will not pay for you under the SR/RV. It may be tough to reconcile but the new plan says that any financial burden incurred by you will not be paid by US taxpayers—even if we once paid for those with fake ID's in the past, when many more people were in the shadows.

Sunshine with no shadows

Celebrate the Sun. The Resident Visa Plan is a sunshine plan. Enjoy your tan. There are no shadows. Everything is in the open. Just do not ask American taxpayers to pay anything for your sustenance.

Charitable organizations such as the Salvation Army, Catholic Social Services, Jewish Charities of America, National Association of Free and Charitable Clinics. Shriners and St. Jude's Hospital to name a few, as well as many others are ready to help Americans or guests who need help with all types of issues. Government will not make payments to Resident Visa Holders under the SR/RV. Period!

Here is a list of a few important notions that will help make this plan work for interloper and American taxpayer alike

- Visa Holders live and work freely in the US
- Visa Holders must be employed
- Visa Holders must have healthcare
- Citizens will no longer pay for EMTALA
    - Emergency Medical Treatment & Active Labor Act

- SR/RV may use EMTALA as all US citizens but must pay for it, when billed, just as a citizen.
- EMTALA and all such emergency debt may be added to the EAR
- Obamacare or its replacement w/o subsidies must be made available for guests to purchase… no freebies.
- Etc.

The accountability database, ACCT, will contain an Electronic Accountability Record (EAR), similar to an Electronic Health Record (EHR), or an Electronic Medical Record (EMR). This is a unique idea for a government that likes to give one person's dollars to another without ever keeping track of how much was given to whom. Today, regardless of the service, there is never a request for a payback of taxpayer dollars. Why is this?

Payback is a b—tch

Politicians like to gain favor by spending Mary's dollars to give five different Joe's a break. They buy votes with all of our dollars. They rarely have sympathy for those they help. They hold them accountable for no payback—just a lifelong silent commitment to keep the villain politicians in office for having provided the favors. Even Mary and Joe who benefit, think the system is corrupt.

This corrupt system kills us domestically as it is the norm in our welfare system and it is killing us on the immigration front. It not only costs taxpayers as much as $500 Billion per year, it serves as a huge magnet for the world to ignore our borders, and simply "come on down!"

Once the incentive for freebies is gone, only the productive members of any other society will try to come to America. The quality of our new citizens and our guests will increase. If they do not like America, their applications for residence or Resident Visa status will be rejected because we do not like people who do not like our country.

Valid in Health Information Technology Systems Also!

Today in the Health Information Technology realm, computerized database systems already can accommodate Electronic Medical Records (EMRs) and Electronic Health Records (EHRs). Even in the domestic health industry with so many payments coming from government in the form of welfare for health purposes and EMTALA, I would propose a new record type called the Electronic Accountability Record (EAR). But that is not the focus of this book. I have mentioned it multiple times as the SR/RV cannot exist well for very long without an EAR system.

Let's define the three databases which we have been lightly discussing since we began this book adventure. Two are currently used in all Health Management Software in doctors' offices and in hospitals, clinics and pharmacies. The third is being proposed in this book to accommodate those Resident Visa Holders who simply cannot pay off a huge debt in a short period of time.

- EMR Electronic Medical Record – Doctors or health services provider's local database patient record
- EHR Electronic Health Record – Doctors or providers sharable database patient record kept in a national database [in the sky!]
- EAR Electronic Accountability Record—Doctors or providers' sharable database and / or an immigration database of financial data used to capture and store all paid and unpaid charges & payments [in the sky!]

There would be an EAR record today if the SR/RV were implemented. Its data would be housed within the ACCT database in the Resident Visa Holder Program.

The US medical system has no such financial database because everything is free if it is sponsored by government. That means it is paid by taxpayers who have no say.

Should there be no accountability to the taxpayers?

Before we modify the US Visa Systems to accommodate a system for Resident Visa Holders, rather than deport everybody that owes the US a dime, and never collect anything, we must assure that we can capture the amounts due to the US Treasury or other government treasuries such as those in states, counties, and municipalities. Why should the services provided to any illegal foreign national not be on his or her record so that one day, the fees for those services can be re-payed?

The best example to show the value of a financial accountability notion being built into all government systems is the case of a lottery winner who has been on government care and cash all their lives. With no accountability system as we propose, even Uncle Sam has no idea how much was spent on the care and feeding of such an individual lotte7

How many dollars or in-kind welfare are received?

And so, when their ship comes in, they know there is no need to pay back anything to the fine taxpayers who helped get them through the tough times in their lives. They know that the taxpayers did not keep track of anything, and there is never a need to pay anything back... Nothing.... Ever...per year or per ever?

You may have read about cases in which the converse is true however. What about a massive lottery winner, who continues to collect their government benefits and they never look back and they never pay anything back. Worse than that, they never think of telling the government to shut off their benefits because they are now OK!

Intrinsically, we all know this is wrong. However, I would never suggest that when a positive life changing event occurs that government step in and ruin the parade completely. Does the lottery win make the new millionaire an elite? Possibly, but so what? I see no problem in raining on say half of the parade for big lottery winners, who owe society for their personal care over many years. But not all!

Why should a future lottery winner at a minimum not have to pay back what he or she has received in benefits over the years? They will not be inclined to ever pay them back unless we, the givers keep track of our "gifts." Lottery winners are not the only ones who should pay back.

Is everything free?

All receivers should pay back something for what they received when they needed help the most. Why should they not want to? Government until today has implicitly told them it was a gift from their neighborhood politician. Hopefully, the President Trump Administration will correct this misimpression of justice.

By the way, to repeat, in this instance, I would limit the government's take to 50% of lottery winnings to pay back lifestyles paid by taxpayers even if the winner owed more.

Who would ever play the lottery, theoretically beneficial to poor Americans, if all the proceeds went to our wasteful government officials?

Additionally, people recovering from disabilities that put them on the dole. As they recover, and as their fortunes change, it would not be bad for them to be asked to pay back something—let's say on a yearly basis to ease the strain on taxpayers. I think if we only asked them by name, they would help the rest of the unfortunate. Of course, it is vital to have all names and records.

So, the bottom line is that the ACCT / EAR database whatever you choose to label it, will be built to track unpaid taxes, expenses—all debts owed in the Resident Visa Holder process. It does not matter if it was OK or not OK debt; earned or unearned; paid or unpaid. The day has come for it to be repaid.

The Resident Visa renewal on-site appearance can be used to assure that all former interloper debt is paid. The fee each year must be paid with no excuses. Either the guest makes full payment or an approved partial payment of their EAR balance, or they may be put on a USCIS approved payment plan. Or, of course, there is always voluntary deportation.

If former interlopers refuse to pay what the agents think is a proper amount or if they refuse to pay anything at all towards their fines, and back taxes, they are candidates for a deportation that must happen. It must be a risky proposition for the former interloper in order to assure their compliance and payment.

Additional charges may be assessed by the interviewers based on the behavior of the interviewee.

For example, if the aspirant gives a hard-working USCIS agent or a stand-in from the Post Office a hard time when calculating debt, taxes, etc., Why should that not cost the aspirant an extra fine? T

The cost for any extra interview time should be paid by the aspirant at an appropriate cost rate. The computer program may advise the interviewer that an additional fee needs to be collected right then and there.

In every instance in which an aspirant or a guest indiscriminately and inappropriately takes more interviewer time than deemed appropriate, their EAR should absorb an extra charge or they should pay the charge immediately.

These records are kept assuring payback over time, and so in the long run, there are no costs to the US taxpayer.

The database records of registrants should "never" be deleted. I would think that a record deletion should need proof of death for at least 50 years in the grave. The US objective is to collect for all debts from the debtor or the beneficiary of the debts.

Taxpayers want a nice fair deal for interlopers that does not involve the taxpayer having to pay a dime. That is the purpose of this book. If SR/RV status individuals want to take advantage of American taxpayers in ways not shown in this book, this scribe suggests the SR/RV pays the toll and then some.

Chapter 14 Jobs for Americans First

Americans don't benefit when jobs are taken

The "Citizens for Laws" group notes that “For every 100 illegal aliens who find jobs in the US, 65 American workers are displaced.” Just this past February 2015, in the news, they announced that for each job that has been created since 2008, two jobs have gone to illegal foreign nationals.

Somebody, who is supposed to be representing Americans, is not doing their job. Neither Congress nor President Obama has chosen to stop the erosion of opportunity and reality for Americans. That is why Donald J. Trump was elected as our new President.

Congress and the past President did not care that there are precious few jobs and those that are advertised are quickly taken by illegal foreign nationals for slave wages. Quite frankly, Americans are sick of foreigners taking American jobs.

Why are foreigners able to take American jobs so easily? Are Americans bad employees? No! It is pure economics. Since there was no workplace enforcement of the immigration laws by the Obama Administration, employers were permitted to pay illegal workers illegal wages or whatever they want, and there was no retribution. In fact, once would be more correct to say there was encouragement.

Moreover, employers know how to game the system. They further protect themselves from the remote possibility of arrest by having no employees. Instead they hire contractors who then hire illegal foreign nationals and everything is OK for them, and only them. This must be stopped and will be stopped with the Donald J. Trump—Master Builder Resident Visa Plan, as soon as somebody shows this book to the Master Builder. The problem of course is that companies can appear to have no employees on the books when and if the government comes checking.

Businesses benefit with illegal employees

Why are businesses so anxious to hire foreigners? That too is easy to answer. Illegal foreign nationals, as well as those here legally on special work visas will work for peanuts rather than go back to their home countries for work. This drives wages down for all Americans in all industries where this practice is permitted and immigration is not enforced.

When the price of everything is going up, it makes little sense that median family income is dropping rapidly. Illegal immigration is a major issue for American family economics. The wages of Americans ought to be rising with the price of food, clothing, and all goods and services upon which Americans depend.

But, because Americans must accept lower wages or be unemployed as a result of the influx of interlopers, the home economies of lower and lower middle-class workers are not in good shape regardless of how well Wall Street may be doing.

Of course, there are great plaudits for the successes of the fracking industry and all the employees being hired in this industry. But, it is the last successful industry in America. Americans know President Trump will make this better. The Resident Visa Plan is a tool that can make it better quicker.

Guess what? The Obama administration was willing to shut down the fracking industry in an instant if it could. Worse than that, instead of opposing Obama in destroying these great jobs, which assure oil and natural gas independence, your Democratic Senators would have support him 100%. Now that Mr. Trump is in office, we need to get rid of the Democrats and the RINOS next. They let Obama get away with hurting Americans. We owe them no allegiance.

With fracking and actually with our poor economy, gas and oil prices are almost back to where they were when President Obama took office. Ironically, though he is against drilling anywhere in the US, and he hates fossil fuels, this marginal President took credit for the recent lowering of gas prices. He is one of the few humans alive who actually does get to have it both ways. It makes at least half of all Americans so happy that he is gone. Good Riddance!

There are many statistics to prove that taxpayers are paying for illegal aliens to live here to the tune of $100 Billion to $500 Billion per year. It is all illegal but with no enforcement, anything goes. To make matters worse, corrupt Congressmen such as Chuck Schumer, Marco Rubio and the Gang of Eight were willing to add a $6.3 Trillion lifetime price tag for taxpayers if their bill were passed in 2013.

Our Senators are out of touch with Americans. Obama would have passed it. As long as we have President Trump, we should be safe for the next eight years.

Taxpayers have not only been paying for those taking their jobs, they have been suffering suppressed wages to the tune of another $200 Billion per year as a result of interlopers accepting substantially lower wages, thereby lowering the wage amount hiring threshold.

Chapter 15 Speak English!

English and American

English and American are different languages. The English people dominated the colonies and so their language dominated the New World. American is very much like English and so Americans still say we speak English. I am of Irish descent, I speak English, not Gaelic, because English is the language of my country.

In colonial days, most of the citizens of the country chose to speak English as fluently as possible. Those, who did not speak the language of the country did not gain the great fortunes provided by the country. The same is true today. Learn English or stay behind and suffer until you can talk and understand the language.

Americans should not want to keep people in the country in the SR/RV who refuse to learn our language.

Any citizen of the US with a few generations behind them knows that our grandparents may not have spoken English well, but they quickly learned the language to support their families in the New World. Only recently, when the notion that being a foreigner qualified for the mythical and politically correct positive notion of being diverse, did language become a stumbling block. Most regular Americans who are not part of the elite know this is pure bunkum.

English cannot be optional

As I see it; it is not optional to know and speak English unless you want to be a failure in life. Not requiring English as our language is like Congress condemning those who receive the least remuneration for their work to stay in such jobs forever.

Not speaking English is like trying to program the internal parts of a computer using a spoken language when the machine understands only machine language. You will fail and those who try to speak foreign tongues in America will fail. It is a given. One would think that Congress does not want green card holders and foreign guests to fail?

You cannot be a worthy American if you do not try to speak the language of our country. English, not Irish (Gaelic) nor Syrian, a language in which I know a few words, has been our language regardless of our native languages, and regardless of our countries of origin.

Everybody learned English and nobody complained as our nation gained its strength as the melting pot. We all needed to speak a common language so we knew what our conversation partners were talking about.

Diversity divides; it does not unite

Americans were trained by the patriotic schools of our country that nation of origin did not matter because, after all, we were and are all Americans.

Diversity divides; it does not unite. We are the United States of America, and each one of us, who has spent some real time here in this country, along with the many who have researched our history, know that America, until the eight Obama years in recent history has had its own unique culture.

Diversity is a major divider, and so it is a prized notion for those Marxists in control who clearly are pushing US down the path of failure.

The skin of America is red, white, yellow, brown, black and beautiful mixes of all colors. America has no national skin color. Skin color does not matter at all in America, especially as our nation has aged and matured.

Some Marxist progressives seem unhappy unless they can bring in new immigrants from Ireland and Syria and Norway, and Libya, and tell them they do not have to melt into anything. They encourage a diversity—not a unity of purpose for Americans and for our country. Not speaking English is another divider of people in the US.

Marxist progressive Democrats do not like American freedoms. Their ideas were not good in the 1600's and 1700's and they are not good today.

Strength comes with unity

They are wrong! The strength of our country comes from all US citizens who at one time, way in the past, looked at each other in the melting pot and decided to melt for the sake of unity of purpose. Our strength does not come from those who choose to remain aligned with their past; their country of origin; or a divisive ideology. It comes from people choosing to be practicing Americans, and eventually real Americans.

That can work also when a person is in Resident Visa Holder status. And, so English is our language and if you want to be part of this great country, learn English and speak English, especially when those who do not understand your foreign tongue are close by. That is respectful of America.

English – the Language of America!

The Americans that I know are fully united in their support for an English language requirement as part of any immigration legislation. Newer polls suggest that nearly 76 percent of adults believe that illegal immigrants should speak and understand English before ever gaining a shred of legal status. The Pew Research / USA Today poll is the source.

Congress does not take this notion of a national language seriously enough as their main concern is always reelection. Borders, culture, and language are important for America. Congress must put some notions on the table requiring new immigrants (no laws currently apply to interlopers other than deportation) to be proficient in English or at least be enrolled in a program to learn English.

The Pew poll also sheds light on a key fight between conservative Republicans and immigration reform supporters concerning whether the proposal should secure the border "first" before granting legal status to immigrants in the United States illegally.

The poll shows Americans are divided on the issue. Until Lou Barletta spoke up in a big way in the Halls of Congress recently, the membership had been completely ineffective on border security. Additionally, President Obama did all he could to remove any border restrictions—even though the US cannot absorb all seven Billion members of the world's population.

By the way, it is difficult to swear an oath of allegiance in the national language of a country if you cannot speak the language. And so, in the Resident Visa Plan proposed legislation, English is designated as the official US language. It should have been done many years ago! Why not? As your local politicians. They made it so.

In summary, an Resident Visa Holder must learn to speak some English in the first two years.

A test will be given after the second year and one additional year as a guest until after the third year. At each renewal period, a test shall be given and at the end of the third year, the Resident Visa Holder must pass a comprehensive English test; have Resident Visa Holder status revoked; or pay for remedial English training classes on an exception basis.

Oath of allegiance

The Resident Visa Plan includes the requirement of an Oath of Allegiance to the United States of America. Aspirants must swear a special oath of allegiance to the US after the first year prior to the renewal interview.

The oath itself must be modeled after the US citizenship oath. It must be designed so as not to permit some smaller allegiance to home, but the language has to place US interests above all competing interests. It is the aspirant's choice as to whether to be an Resident Visa Holder under the US terms and conditions.

Anybody who hates the US and expresses that view in any Resident Visa Plan interview or renewal must be deported immediately. Their families must then be scrutinized for potential terrorists. We do not want anybody who hates the US as a guest—ever!

The first question in the aspirant interview should ask if the aspirant hates the US. All who answer in the affirmative should not get one more minute in the country and should be deported right then from the interview station. It is not a joke!

SR/RV solves a big problem for US and interlopers

The Resident Visa Plan solves the problem of 20million to 60 million interlopers illegally residing in the US. It favors Americans as opposed to foreigners and it assures that the immigration reform demands of Americans are met!

With so many human beings living in the shadows, and so many Americans being hurt by a lack of jobs and a lower standard of living due to the lack of enforcement of sound and solid immigration law, the problem begs for a real solution; not a series of tricks to attract illegal voters to one political party or another.

Nobody gets citizenship from participation in the Resident Visa Plan (SR/RV) but the interlopers here in an illegal status do get the opportunity to become real Resident Visa Holders of the United States. This enables them to walk freely and work freely in America without the risk of deportation. That, my friends is a real big deal, and a generous act on the part of the American people for those who are in our country illegally.

A Visa Holder is a type of guest, not an owner.

Wherever an advantage is to go to either an interloper; a registrant; an aspirant; a guest; or an American, the American always comes first in the Resident Visa Holder Pan. Let me repeat that as it is not the way it is today. All advantages must go to American citizens.

Moreover, a guest of the US is not a second class anything. They are guests—nothing more and nothing less. As a guest, they are not citizens or permanent residents and so they do not have the rights of US citizens. And, of course, to become a guest, they must agree and sign on the dotted line that they will abide by all stipulations of being a US annual guest.

No lawsuits will be accepted from any guest about the question of guest status. When an interloper signs on the dotted line during registration, they agree to abide by the rules of the process. When they sign to become an annual guest, they get only the rights in that document, other than natural rights, to which all human beings are entitled.

Consequently, a person in Resident Visa Holder status, besides natural rights from God to life, liberty, and the pursuit of happiness, has only the specific rights as defined in the SR/RV law. Guests must play by strict US rules and they must support themselves & families since there are no freebies permitted in the plan. the Stipend Return / Resident Visa Program includes border security as defined by Congressman Barletta, with the additional notes added in this book.

We leave the substantial thoughts on border security to the Master Builder, President Donald J. Trump. The emphasis area in the Resident Visa Plan portrayed in this book is the millions of interlopers currently living in the shadows or operating under Obama's temporary amnesty, while that still provides protections.

Chapter 16 Birthright Citizenship (Anchor Babies)

Interlopers gain and Americans gain

A look at the costs of not having a Resident Visa plan v having such a plan shows that it is obvious that there will be some special things that can be afforded to help keep families together in their home country. The benefits over time for this program to the National treasury is more than $500 Billion per year. That is huge. This benefit is shared with the families of interlopers so they can be safely resettled in their home countries if they choose to take advantage of stipends which are readily available.

For example, a birthright citizen, aka an *anchor baby*, either an adult or through his or her parents can choose to take a $50,000 *birthright citizen stipend* to go back to the parents' home country. When added to the stipends of the mother and father, for a family of three, this would amount to a $90,000 stipend. Additionally, the US government will assist in settling the family into a safe area of their home country?

A family of six would be given a stipend of $240,000. This is a very lucrative proposition for interlopers with anchor babies. The 20-year cost of an anchor baby in the US is staggering and all could be avoided. The lifetime cost of course is more than three times the 20-year cost $30,000 X 60) = $1.8 million.

The anchor baby with family could start anew in the home country. The family can go back home instead of living in the US, which is a foreign country to them. With their bankroll. the family could become big-shot entrepreneurs in their home country.

There may be families, for example a single mom with one child, that could gain a grub stake of $70,000 to several hundred thousand dollars, depending on the # of children, to start fresh in their home country with their families intact. Why would they want to stay in America with no grand prize? America to them often seems like a foreign land?

What is an *Anchor Baby*?

When interviewed several years ago on Fox, by Greta Van Susteren, when she had her own show, Senator Lyndsey Graham said that "there's another problem we have in this nation that I think is novel and needs to be fixed. If you come across the border illegally and you have a child in America, automatically, that child becomes an American citizen. Under the 14th Amendment, three court cases say there's a constitutional right to that. [Yet, many constitutional scholars refute this assertion.]

“I would like to deal with the 12 million (illegal immigrants) firmly and fairly. You can't stay here on your own terms. You have to learn English. You have to pay fines. You have to get in the back of the line if you want to be a citizen. But I may introduce a constitutional amendment that changes the rules if you have a child here. Birthright citizenship, I think, is a mistake, that we should change our Constitution and say if you come here illegally and you have a child, that child's automatically not a [US]citizen."

Later in the interview, Van Susteren asked Graham, "How realistic is it that you will introduce a constitutional amendment?

Graham replied that he had to because "people come here to have babies. They come here to drop a child. It's called 'drop and leave.' To have a child in America, they cross the border, they go to the emergency room, have a child, and that child's automatically an American citizen. That shouldn't be the case. That attracts people here for all the wrong reasons." [Moreover, the hospital pays for the babies and many are going out of business because they cannot recoup their expenses.]

In a later interview with Van Susteren on Aug. 3 of the same year, Graham once again referred to a "problem where thousands of people are coming across the Arizona-Texas border for the express purpose of having a child in an American hospital so that child will become an American citizen, and they broke the law to get there."

Does being an American mean that Americans all must be chumps for anybody who comes along wanting something? Are we the suckers that will never be given an even break simply because we like mankind and everybody that learns quickly learns that it is a quick way into the wallet of every caring American. Nobody, who has exploited this misguided system, has ever paid anything back to the Americans that helped assure their baby's safety in America.

The idea of the Resident Visa Plan is to help those stuck in America doing meaningless labor for peanuts. It is a plan to help Americans subjugated to the effects of a new but clandestine wage scale that comes before all minimum wages, for which they cannot compete.

Chapter 17 Fees & Fines for Resident Visa Holders & Employers

Interlopers & employers are declared GUILTY!

Interlopers could not have lasted more than a week or two in the US without getting jobs someplace. The risk that employers took in hiring them under the minimum wage, especially in the 1980's and 1990's was huge. Therefore, a rational thinking being must conclude that the rewards of hiring employees in illegal status, at times when punishment was an option, were significant. Employers made a killing having illegal employees working for them for peanuts. It was worth the risk. Now, they must pay.

And, so in this chapter, we make suggestions about the types of crimes that require punishment of a sort (fines) for both interlopers, who have gotten to enjoy America's freedoms and protections and many other benefits; and for employers who made a killing off their backs. It is now time to pay the piper.

I suggest that Americans feel no guilt or shame about getting something back into the treasury for all the years we have been whooped by interlopers and employers, with the willing hand of our elected Congressmen and Senators, who assured that Americans would lose at every turn.

Fees and fines help pay for implementation

All of the numbers in the following charts are estimates based on facts. They are designed to be reasonable. America should be able to collect most of these fees and fines with no problem over time. There will be some startup burps but this is all feasible. Only the person who says they can't is right 100% of the time.

When fines cannot be paid immediately, USCIS agents will have the option to permit the debt to be carried in the interloper's EAR in the ACCT (debt database). A similar record must be set up for companies who once hired an illegal alien worker. The Resident Visa Holder EAR record is created at when the interloper gets a passport. It is completed during the aspirant interviews. From then on, it can be updated with appropriate charges, fines, and fees.

For at least three years of Resident Visa implementation, until the Resident Visa Holder passes the required tests, no dollars should be collected in fees and fines. However, they will be accrued in the database. This will help the program get kicked off properly.

The following fines are proposed to be assessed upon interlopers for crimes and misdemeanors against the American people. There is no amnesty.

Type of Fine	Amount of Fine
• Interloper one-time fine	$2,000
• Fake ID fine	$500
• Medical services fine	$200
• Demography not updated	$200
• Failure to get passport	$5000 + deportation
• Failure to apply for SR/RV	$1000 + deportation
• Failure to renew	$1000 + deportation

For those who fail to get a passport and are discovered and apprehended, they may pay a $5,000 fine immediately, and immediately apply for a passport or self-deport. If they take no action to move forward in the program, the government will sign them up for an all-expenses paid trip to their home country with the costs added to their EAR.

The Resident Visa Holder or deportee pays all processing fees for any special considerations. American taxpayers pay nothing.

Employer fines

Without complicit employers in this major perpetration brought on the American people, there would be no such interloper problem in America today. The greed of businesses for increased profits brought big and small companies alike to the point where they felt it worth the risk to their business to hire interlopers in illegal status for slave wages rather than hire Americans for a proper wage. Companies have made millions in excessive profits due to their callous disregard for American laws and the effect of their actions on their fellow citizens.

Therefore, in terms of paying back the United States, the companies of America that have employed foreign nationals in illegal status need to pay their fair share back to America for the years and years and years of profits they gained on the backs of Americans and the poor souls they employed.

Americans have either lost good paying jobs or have been forced to take substantially lower paying jobs as companies fattened their bottom lines. I am a tried and true capitalist but this perpetration on foreign nationals and on Americans did not have to be. It was pure greed.

It was the answer that US based companies had to those of their peers who could offshore work. It is almost impossible to offshore services or production jobs that require immediate employee intervention or access to perishable material. But, the Turkish phrase captures what they did: " If the mountain won't come to you, you must go to the mountain."

Just as we permit the Resident Visa Holders to put some of their debt into an EAR for tracking, the SR/RV program will provide a similar means of tracking for the debt owed by the companies who have gained for far too many years as Americans and foreign interlopers suffered from their greed.

And so, a substantial employer fine is recommended to be imposed if as little as one and as many as a company-full of interloper employees / contractors have ever been used by the organization since the Reagan amnesty of 1986. The fine would be added first to the

Employer Electronic Accountability Record, another form of the EAR that we can refer to as the EEAR in the ACCT database.

The fine amount per company is to be determined at the company interview/audit. In addition to the fine, companies will pay for the time expended in the audit. Additional levies / penalties will be executed if the employers choose not to tell the whole truth.

Please note, this fine will not punish innocent companies. Any company that hired as few as one interloper is guilty so most businesses in the US today are guilty, plain and simple. Companies may appeal the guilty verdict by proving beyond speculation that their policy and their results were 100% in compliance with the SR/RV plan—in other words, not one interloper was employed by the company for any length of time from 1986 on.

Companies that are guilty will all be punished at the same rate per active employee in any immigration status. They will be fined proportionately to their employee base. If zero employees have been in an illegal status from 1986 through 2017, then the employer will not be fined at all.

However, if one or more employees were in interloper status, the fine amount itself is based on the number of employees working for the company as of 2017, not the year of the infraction(s).

To repeat, the rule for whether a company is fined or not is simple: "If one employee in the company or in any of the bought–out or derivative companies in the organization, was in an illegal status over the thirty-year+ period, the company is fined."

What are the employer **fine** amounts?

- Fine -- $2000 per current active employee
- Six Months to Pay Fine
- Late Payment (10% per month)
- No Payment / no reason – 4X Fine payable immediately
- Company may request a good-faith payment plan

Fair employer fines raise substantial revenue

Category ranges and estimated potential revenue totals to pay back Americans for this travesty are shown in the Employer Fines / Fees summary after a few more charts. First let's summarize the SR/RV fees and fines again and then show the employer fees and fines. The overriding goal is that this plan should cost the taxpayers zero. Corporations have been paying zero while the taxpayers have been carrying the load for far too long.

Americans with some background in corporate finance as well as adept investors know that U.S. companies have more than $2 Trillion overseas. This is per an analysis that paints a bleak picture of whether that money will ever make its way to the US. The study also suggests that there would be limited economic impact even if it does. I tend to think it would make a big difference. President Trump is expected to bring this revenue back to America to be declared and taxed appropriately.

I can see some good plans being built to bring some of that capital back to help pay the debt that will be owed by corporations for having once hired illegal foreign nationals. There is lots of money overseas. If it were brought back to pay fines and fees, I would suspect a mutually beneficial deal could be worked out.

Fees: Resident Visa Plan	Fees
• Passport Fee	$140
• Resident Visa Fee	$160
• Annual Renewal (Estimate)	$100

<u>Fees: Employers who have used 1 interloper within 30 years</u>
All employers in this status must pay estimated first year's fees

- Company registration (mostly online) $1000
- Reg. Interview per location 1 time $5000
- Verification hardware per loc. / year $1000
- Online Connection per location / year $1000
- Annual renewal incl. 1st year per loc. $1000
- IRS Interview One Time $5000
- Total first-time fees per location **$14000**

- Employers who choose to go all American pay $0.00
  - In fees in future years

$14,000 is the proper employer amount per location as noted above. The full employer analysis is shown in subsequent pages.

Sample revenue chart from employer fees and fines

The summary charts demonstrate potential total US government total revenue (fines, fees, taxes). It presupposes that at some point, every employer has hired at least one interloper. The government is not about to determine how many interlopers over a thirty-year period were hired. One interloper hired indicates guilt.

Thus, one hired interloper means a business pays the fine at their level of potential involvement, which is based on # of potential interloper employees (i.e. their current employee count). They may pay all hearing costs to prove they never hired an interloper and they will be exonerated from payment if found not guilty

Estimated employer fines & fees.

Let's see how much this would cost businesses that have enjoyed unfettered access to workers in an illegal status for as many as thirty years. That is another way of saying that they made untold millions of dollars by choosing not to hire Americans for American work. Do not feel sorry for their huge fines because they made huge amounts during this period.

There are an estimated 6 million employers in the US

Employer Fees Summary – all employers (US Revenue)

Employers in US—approximately 5,809,833
Initial Fees ($14000) X 5809833 = $81,337,662,000
Annual Fees ($2000) X 5809833 = $11,619,666,000

- $81,337,662,000 one-time fees
- $11,619,666,000 annual fees
    - If company chooses to continue to use already employed Resident Visa Holders.

This is a Big Deal and a Big Fine

The following charts summarizes potential total revenue from employer fines. If an employer never hired an interloper, there is no fine. Moreover, none of the fees listed above for 1st time apply. To give us an idea of the fines, we have assumed in the calculations that within a thirty-year window, all employers hired interlopers. If a business hired interlopers and it is now out of business, the prior owners owe the fine unless its obligations have been assumed by the new business owner if the business still exists in any form.

- Total fines = $320 Billion from all employers combined
- Employers have received benefits well beyond $2,000 per illegal immigrant.
- If one illegal immigrant is declared, the full fine is in effect.
- Add to this about 92 $Billion in fees from above

Total first year employer fees and fines = $413,057,328,000.00

Yes, the total is 413 + $Billion

The detail behind this amount is in this chart.

The purpose of this chart is to show the estimated fine cost for employers in various categories of # of employees. Congress will decide if these numbers are the ones they will use but these are more than fair. Think of all the pain their actions caused Americans and the poor living conditions they forced on vulnerable foreign interlopers.

This chart, which is accurate enough to use at the profits gained by employee exploitation were far greater than the fine par company. I would recommend that we use these figures to assess the fines. The sooner the better. If Congress thinks that employers deserve to pay back employees even more as this chart shows numbers at a substantially lower rate than actual, then I would be OK if the Congress raised these fines.

Estimated employer fines & fees (shown at substantially lower rate)

Category Range	Appx Mean# Employees in Category Range	# of US Employers in Category Range	# of US Employees in Category Range	Fine perEmp. $2000.00	Fees -- Reg IRS Tools, etc
				Fine per category	
1 to 10	3	4,600,000	13,800,000	$27,600,000,000	
11 to 100	30	1,100,000	33,000,000	$66,000,000,000	
101 to 500	200	90,000	18,000,000	$36,000,000,000	
501 to 5000	1,250	18,000	22,500,000	$45,000,000,000	
5001 to 100000	37,000	1,800	66,600,000	$133,200,000,000	
100,001 to 250,000	125,000	18	2,250,000	$4,500,000,000	
250,001 to 2,000,000	260,000	15	3,900,000	$7,800,000,000	
Totals			160,050,000	$320,100,000,000	
Total US Labor Force	160,000,000				
Total # US Businesses				5,809,833	$14,000
Total Reg & IRS Fee				$81,337,662,000.00	
Annual Business Fees				$11,619,666,000.00	
Total Fees 1st year				$92,957,328,000.00	
Total Fees/Fines YR 1				$413,057,328,000.00	

Please gaze at the chart.

You can figure this chart out as the captions are clear. It is unbelievable that so many corporations made so many millions by stiffing illegal immigrants upon arrival to America. Shame on them. It is OK to fine them to get back a small fortune of their gains and their lack of reporting violations against Americans.

Summary

The Resident Visa Plan takes interlopers out of the shadows and makes Americans the kings and queens of their own country. It defines terms under which we will accept guests and it makes us a sovereign country again. Guest never vote; never take benefits; never become citizens; never get hired for a job before an American citizen.

Deportations will be minimized but will occur as an enforcement mechanism. The SR/RV system will be designed so that it can readily accommodate visa holders and over-stayers as well as permanent residents. With proper design and programming, only one database will need to be searched by agents to find a foreigner in any status.

Look at the numbers. This plan makes big financial sense for America and it puts Americans on top again where we belong.

Thank you for your attention.

LETS GO PUBLISH! Books by Brian Kelly

(Sold at Amazon.com, and Kindle.).

The Bill of Rights By Founder James Madison Refresh *your knowledge of the specific rights granted to all*
Defeating America's Career Politicians Corrupt career politicians are killing America
Winning Back America: The play by play recommendation to steal the country from bad politicos
Great Players in Army Football Great Army Football played by great players..
Great Coaches in Army Football Army's coaches are all great.
Great Moments in Army Football Army Football at its best.
Great Moments in Florida Gators Football **Gators** Football from the start. This is the book.
Great Moments in Clemson Football **CU** Football at its best. This is the book.
Great Moments in Florida Gators Football **Gators** Football from the start. This is the book. **The Constitution Companion.** A Guide to Reading and Comprehending the Constitution
The Constitution by Hamilton, Jefferson, & Madison – Big type and in English
PATERNO: The Dark Days After Win # 409. Sky began to fall within days of win # 409.
JoePa 409 Victories: Say No More! Winningest Division I-A football coach ever
American College Football: The Beginning From before day one football was played.
Great Coaches in Alabama Football Challenging the coaches of every other program!
Great Coaches in Penn State Football the Best Coaches in PSU's football program
Great Players in Penn State Football The best players in PSU's football program
Great Players in Notre Dame Football The best players in ND's football program
Great Coaches in Notre Dame Football The best coaches in any football program
President Donald J. Trump, Master Builder: Solving the Student Debt Crisis!
President Donald J. Trump, Master Builder: It's Time for Seniors to Get a Break!
President Donald J. Trump, Master Builder: Healthcare & Welfare Accountability
President Donald J. Trump, Master Builder: "Make America Great Again"
President Donald J. Trump, Master Builder: The Annual Guest Plan
Great Players in Alabama Football from Quarterbacks to offensive Linemen Greats!
Great Moments in Alabama Football AU Football from the start. This is the book.
Great Moments in Penn State Football PSU Football, start--games, coaches, players,
Great Moments in Notre Dame Football ND Football, start, games, coaches, players
Four Dollars & Sixty-Two Cents—A Christmas Story That Will Warm Your Heart!
My Red Hat Keeps Me on The Ground. Darraggh's Red Hat is magical
Seniors, Social Security & the Minimum Wage. Things seniors need to know.
How to Write Your First Book and Publish It with CreateSpace
The US Immigration Fix--It's all in here. Finally, an answer.
I had a Dream IBM Could be #1 Again The title is self-explanatory
WineDiets.Com Presents The Wine Diet Learn how to lose weight while having fun.
Wilkes-Barre, PA; Return to Glory Wilkes-Barre City's return to glory
Geoffrey Parsons' Epoch... The Land of Fair Play Better than the original.
The Bill of Rights 4 Dummmies! This is the best book to learn about your rights.
Sol Bloom's Epoch ...Story of the Constitution The best book to learn the Constitution
America 4 Dummmies! All Americans should read to learn about this great country.
The Electoral College 4 Dummmies! How does it really work?
The All-Everything Machine Story about IBM's finest computer server.
Brian has written 128 books. Others can be found at amazon.com/author/brianwkelly

Made in the USA
Monee, IL
04 November 2026

67385037R00105